OFF THE MAP

Reel Spirituality Monograph Series
Series Description

The Reel Spirituality Monograph Series features a collection of theoretically precise yet readable essays on a diverse set of film-related topics, each of which makes a substantive contribution to the academic exploration of Theology and Film. The series consists of two kinds of works: 1) popular-level introductions to key concepts in and practical applications of the Theology and Film discipline, and 2) methodologically rigorous investigations of theologically significant films, filmmakers, film genres, and topics in cinema studies. The first kind of monograph seeks to introduce the world of Theology and Film to a wider audience. The second seeks to expand the academic resources available to scholars and students of Theology and Film. In both cases, these essays explore the various ways in which "the cinema" (broadly understood to include the variety of audio-visual storytelling forms that continues to evolve along with emerging digital technologies) contributes to the overall shape and trajectory of the contemporary cultural imagination. The larger aim of producing both scholarly and popular-level monographs is to generate a number of resources for enthusiasts, undergraduate and graduate students, and scholars. As such, the Reel Spirituality Monograph Series ultimately exists to encourage the enthusiast to become a more thoughtful student of the cinema and the scholar to become a more passionate viewer.

Previously published in the series:
Davidson, Elijah Lynn, *How to Talk to a Movie: Movie-Watching as a Spiritual Exercise*

Forthcoming in the series:
Wells, Justin, *From Actuality to Ecstasy: Documentary Film and the Quest for Truth*

OFF THE MAP

Freedom, Control, and the Future in Michael Mann's Public Enemies

Niles Schwartz
series foreword by Elijah Lynn Davidson

CASCADE *Books* · Eugene, Oregon

OFF THE MAP
Freedom, Control, and the Future in Michael Mann's *Public Enemies*

Reel Spirituality Monograph Series 2

Copyright © 2018 Niles Schwartz. All rights reserved. Except for brief quotations in critical publications or reviews, no part of this book may be reproduced in any manner without prior written permission from the publisher. Write: Permissions, Wipf and Stock Publishers, 199 W. 8th Ave., Suite 3, Eugene, OR 97401.

Cascade Books
An Imprint of Wipf and Stock Publishers
199 W. 8th Ave., Suite 3
Eugene, OR 97401

www.wipfandstock.com

PAPERBACK ISBN: 978-1-5326-3658-5
HARDCOVER ISBN: 978-1-5326-3660-8
EBOOK ISBN: 978-1-5326-3659-2

Cataloging-in-Publication data:

Names: Schwartz, Niles
Title: Off the map : freedom, control, and the future in Michael Mann's *Public Eniemies* / by Niles Schwartz.
Description: Eugene, OR : Cascade Books, 2018 | Series: Reel Spirituality Monograph Series | Includes bibliographical references.
Identifiers: ISBN 978-1-5326-3658-5 (paperback) | ISBN 978-1-5326-3660-8 (hardcover) | ISBN 978-1-5326-3659-2 (ebook)
Subjects: LCSH: Mann, Michael (Michael Kenneth)—Criticism and interpretation. | Motion pictures—Social aspects.
Classification: LCC PN1998.3.M3645 S23 2018 (PRINT) | LCC PN1998.3.M3645 (EBOOK)

Manufactured in the U.S.A.   JUNE 8, 2018

CONTENTS

SERIES FOREWORD

Elijah Davidson

In 1851, a former sailor and budding novelist published a book about whaling that was, upon publication, almost entirely disregarded. Small wonder, the book is an ungainly thing, more cetology and whaling manual than story. The multitudinous technical passages are stitched together by thin narrative fragments concerning a crazed captain and his strange crew, and the story is told by a narrator who seems intent on not revealing himself. And every bit of it, the encyclopedic sections and the plot-driven ones, all leap compulsively, mawkishly to the metaphysical.

Moby-Dick, or The Whale is a book that tries to get as close as possible to one thing—whaling—to discover all things. The book is a chase story, of a man, Ishmael/Herman Melville after a profession; of a crew, the *Pequod*'s, after its captain, Ahab; of Ahab after the white whale, Moby Dick; and of them all after truth, purpose, ambition, belonging, order, prosperity, freedom, self-determination, peace. The book is about the economy (the whaling industry then the equivalent of petroleum industry today), technology, camaraderie, professionalism, politics, religion (the limits thereof), globalism, science, and the particularity of the American identity. It is about god, but not the god that Melville learned about in the Dutch Reformed Church where he was baptized as an infant. It's about whether or not another god is possible and, if not, why the whale?

Moby-Dick, or The Whale is not a spiritual text in the traditional sense, clearly not in the Christian doctrinal sense but also not in the sense of the popular secular spirituality of Melville's time, Transcendentalism. In its excoriation of Ahab's monomania, it lays waste to the idea that any one man can achieve anything but destruction through self-reliance. Even the novel's famous opening line—"Call me Ishmael."—establishes the novel as alt-Judeo-Christian and separates the reader from any internal life the narrator privately cultivates. A far cry from Genesis's "very good" creation or Emerson's naturalistic reveries, in *Moby-Dick*, the natural world is ambivalent to humanity at best and more likely malicious toward it. Ahab's obsession is presented as evidence that people corrupt institutions and not the other way around. The subjective is censured—Ahab cannot perceive the whale even when it is barreling toward him. Doggedly, Melville pulls the reader out of her or himself and into the minutia of whaling, like a sailor plucking a drowning man from the sea—the hands-on world, frustratingly quick to sink though it may be, is all that certainly is, the only hope of salvation. Only Ishmael the empiricist survives.

Whatever else it is about, the book is about dissatisfaction with the world as-is and restless searching for something more, and in the end Ishmael and Ahab and the reader are all left devastated and adrift, one amongst the waves, one below them, and the rest abandoned to the non-literary world as suddenly as Melville dropped us into his narrative. *Moby-Dick, or the Whale* leaves us with desire alone. If Augustine is correct, and that which makes us human, essentially—that which sets Ishmael and Ahab and Melville and us apart from the whale—is our restless desire to find satisfaction in something beyond ourselves, in God, then *Moby-Dick, or the Whale* is a spiritual treatise *par excellence*.

Within a decade, Melville's literary career sputtered. He took a job as a customs inspector and held that job for the next nineteen years. He continued to write—publishing small volumes of poetry, mostly, for his family and friends. There is no evidence those final forty years of his life were happy. He drank heavily, abused his wife and children, endured a son's suicide, and kept striving to produce another literary work that would win him popular acclaim. He died in obscurity in 1891. They misspelled his first name in his obituary. *Moby-Dick* was forgotten, and his now second-most lauded work, the novella *Billy Budd*, was unfinished.

Thirty years later, a new generation of literary scholars rediscovered Melville's work as they prepared surveys of American literary history, and their work propelled Melville to new, world-wide renown. Most importantly for our purposes, a young, soon-to-be French Resistance fighter named Jean-Pierre Grumbach was taken with Melville's work and adopted his name as his own. After World War II, the now *nom de guerre*d Jean-Pierre Melville kept the name as his stage name as he began making films.

This new Melville borrowed everything from the old except the sea. As his eponym wrote about the sailors he worked with early in his life, Jean-Pierre Melville made films about cops and robbers of the kind he knew during his Resistance days. And his films are similarly obsessed with the details of process, contemporary masculinity, camaraderie, professionalism, contested religiosity, technology, and all those Melvillian abstract concerns as well, like belonging, ambition, order, freedom, self-determination, purpose and whether or not meaning is achievable given the impenetrability of all things, especially other people. Jean-Pierre Melville's films are also profoundly dissatisfying, building to an exciting climax and then leaving you adrift, not in Ishmael's ocean but amidst the foggy streets of post-war Paris. Ever the Ameriphile, the new Melville's films are riffs on American gangster films, made for popular audiences, featuring movie stars, simply touched with a particular malaise. The new Melville didn't suffer the former's fate – Jean-Pierre was loved. He was a kind of father figure to the filmmakers of the French New Wave.

Michael Mann, the filmmaker whose film, *Public Enemies*, Niles Schwartz investigates in this book, has never publicly confessed a keenness for either Melville. (Once asked about Jean-Pierre by Bilge Ebiri, Mann, ever the Ameriphile himself, likened him to an English band trying to cover Muddy Waters.[1]) However, the similarities between Mann's and Jean-Pierre Melville's films are clear—"cops and robbers" procedurals, interested in the same sociological matters and abstract ideals, as taken with the goodness of professional camaraderie, and scored by the same kind of inescapable dissatisfaction with the world.

In that last case then, Mann's films are as "spiritual" as French, post-war ennui and as *Moby-Dick*, which is to say, not spiritual at all in any traditional sense, ecclesial or secular, but as spiritual as any art ever made in the Augustinian sense. This is a spirituality that is only more pertinent in the Postmodern era that is rooted in deep dissatisfaction with

1. Bilge Ebiri, "Crime in Counterpoint: Michael Mann on his Restored Masterpiece *Heat*." *The Village Voice* (May 8, 2017) http://www.phoenixnewtimes.com/film/crime-in-counterpoint-michael-mann-on-his-restored-masterpiece-heat-9306583.

the proposed meta-narratives of the Modern world . . . but I'm getting ahead of the book you are about to read.

Niles Schwartz's close examination of *Public Enemies* is Melvillian in scope, just film scholarship instead of cetology. He considers almost every moment of the film and every detail included in each frame. Like Melville's metaphysical leaps at the end of each chapter of *Moby-Dick*, Schwartz lets each moment and detail in *Public Enemies* open up into the cosmos of reference and ideas that informs them and shapes both the filmmaker's and the audience's experience of the film. Schwartz's close attention to *Public Enemies* is the kind of scholarship that makes the movie more fascinating than it is on its own, richer. And since to watch one Michael Mann film is, in a way, to watch them all, Schwartz's dealings with *Public Enemies* is sort of a dealing with Mann's entire filmography. Finally, along the way, he manages to make unavoidable something few critics have noted: a correspondence Mann shares with a contemporary filmmaker of more obviously spiritual concerns—Terrence Malick.

Michael Mann is thankfully not nearly as obscured in his later years as Herman Melville was in his, but there is something concerningly loose about his popular appeal. Esteem for Mann feels apt to slip away like one of his thieves when the going gets tough. God, forbid. But if that does happen, perhaps a future scholar will pick up Schwartz's book and rediscover Mann's verve, and a new generation might be inspired by that kind of honest human desire for something more that filters through the ages in Augustine, in Melville, in "Melville," and in Mann.

Elijah Davidson
March 2018

ACKNOWLEDGMENTS

My gratitude to Elijah Davidson and Kutter Calloway at Fuller Seminary's Brehm Center for the Arts, for seeing something in my callow work from years back, this final product hopefully matured with worthwhile insights thanks to time and reflection. Thanks to those who, as friends, teachers, family, and colleagues, influenced me as a moviegoer and so the direction of this text: Joseph Adams, Joey Barsness, Marshall Bolin, Paul Brooke, Carys Church, Anna Eveslage, Ian Flomer, Aaron Gibbons, Liane Hankland, Erik Hoadley, Amy Kalal, Amy Kase, Maria Elena Mahowald, John McGuinness, Rachel Munger, Solveig Nelson, Mike Reynolds, Caroline Royce, J. D. Schwartz, Hannah Steblay, Rachael Thompson, Jeff Turner, Sybil Zink, Naida Zukic, and Fefu the cat. Also, for their encouragement in my development as a critic, my humble thanks and respect to Jon Baskin at *The Point* magazine and Matt Zoller Seitz at RogerEbert.com; and special thanks to Tommy Mischke, the first person to read *Off the Map* in its embryonic form many years ago, and who was the first person to give me a chance in mass media, inviting me to be his on-air radio film critic at WCCO in Minneapolis, though I was hardly ready.

Being the product of those I've read and admired, thanks to the multitude of writers who've inspired me over the years, some as friends, and others from a distance: Ali Arikan, Jim Brunzell, Sean Burns, Jaime Christley, K. Austin Collins, Colin Covert, David Davidson, Paul McGuire Grimes, Eric Henderson, Glenn Kenny, Lex G, Martha Nochimson, Nick Olson, Peter Labuza, Nick Pinkerton, Bill Ryan, Colin Stacy, Ryan Swen, Scout Tafoya, Brian Tallerico, Keith Uhlich, and, with particular emphasis, Bilge Ebiri. Before 2009, I sort of lived in a bubble, and most of these great minds I only became acquainted with thanks to the wonderful world of social media.

Lastly, I'd like to dedicate this book to the memories of Ron Rosenbaum of St. Paul, "Caretaker" Jim Glanzsman of Minneapolis, and Christina Stinnett of Dardanelle, Arkansas.

—Niles Schwartz

INTRODUCTION:
"THE WAY OF THE FUTURE"

Toward the conclusion of Michael Mann's *Public Enemies*, fugitive bank robber John Dillinger (Johnny Depp) sits down under a beam of dusty light to watch a movie. Engrossed by a lurid crime story (*Manhattan Melodrama*), personal memories are prompted to materialize as he optically confronts an uncanny visage. The image in his head is still opaque, but we know exactly what he's seeing because the memory association is happening to us, almost a century later, far away from Dillinger's ground zero. The movie is the medium as the "soul image" of Dillinger's estranged lover Billie Frechette (Marion Cotillard) takes hold of raw material, emulsion cranked through an enormous projector at 24 frames per second, featuring the actress Myrna Loy. The animism reaches through narrative and form. Dillinger has an existential appointment to keep. He walks onto a crowded Chicago street and is shot by federal agents. As if to release his spirit before he dies, he whispers a message. The film ends and, optically inhaling the image into our being, the soul transmigrates through the medium to us as we exit the theater.

A mysterious alchemy plays out between John Dillinger, the film he's watching, and ourselves, a spiritual synthesis set apart from the other "grand syntheses" playing out through the film's milieu of J. Edgar Hoover's encapsulating modern grid subduing and controlling the frontier, and the film's conspicuously digital approach with implications of an increasingly interconnected world, the ramifications of which were announced fifty years ago as Marshall McLuhan spoke of new media as the "technological simulation of consciousness, when the creative process of knowing will be collectively and corporately extended to the whole of human society," our fragmented selves coming together.[1] But what of the ghost, its message whispering through the cracks of the medium, the way John Dillinger evades capture? Through, in, and with the medium is another self, the grail in this alchemy, heightening the leisurely activity of moviegoing to something religious and transformative, a symbolic interaction not necessarily between people, but between human beings and the tools by which images are made and projected.

Stanley Kubrick's *2001: A Space Odyssey* (1968) showed how a reliance on our tools wedge us from nature, but our continuous interface with technology constantly rewrites the terrestrial firmament, tinting and reprogramming windows of perception with new colors, suggesting essential concepts of nature—and ourselves—are more beguiling and paradoxical than once imagined. In his book *A Cinema of Loneliness*, Robert Kolker analyzed Kubrick's whole body of work as the "Tectonics of the Mechanical Man," the austere control of the director's process an ironic complement to his human characters losing control and becoming inferior to the systems they've created. We're transformed through our tools, from a blunt bone to nuclear weapons to artificial intelligence, resetting the cybernetic stage as a vast and complex consensual hallucination to which we belong

1. McLuhan, *Understanding Media*, 3–4.

more than it belongs to us. How do we hang on to ourselves in a virtual Elsinore where the courtly simulacrum is a stuttering zoetrope, unimpeded technological growth altering established notions of the "real" and ethics, the mirrors and masquerades exponentially replicating before we can focus on a single illuminating reflection as the signal-to-noise obfuscates comprehension?

The grand narratives of the self commingle with technological ingenuity primarily through screen interface. So what are we to do with movies, the most regal of those screens? Are we dynamically in dialogue with the moving image, concentrating our gazes and walking away with its mark imprinted in memory, or do we passively absorb it, lapping it up with any number of other consumables, forgetting it as passable waste? Are we building a reflective conscientiousness, or disintegrating as docile observers taking input and moving forth, one flickering image not differentiated from the next? The new millennium's post-odyssey destination is less Kubrick's Star Gate sequence than reality TV and *Dancing With the Stars*.

Sofia Coppola's *The Bling Ring* (2013), a fact-based film about California rich kids invading the homes of screen celebrities, observed (with the director's remarkably coy acuity) how current cultural iconography relates more to the one-dimensional novelty of celebrity than to a viewer's symbiosis with a performance and character. Cameras are everywhere, and the culture of celebrity establishes an ersatz narrative replacing the introspective narratives of fiction, screen avatars remembered not for their art and craft so much as for their spotlight rep on red carpets and tweets. The publicity machine churns out the new cultural canon, entertainment journalism being an essential and distracting subset of the 24-hour news cycle. Those avatars hollowed, the viewers are complicit—and conjoined—in the hollow subject's spiritual crisis. Coppola's previous film *Somewhere* (2011), intimately followed a mid-tier movie star (Stephen Dorff) going through privileged rich-and-famous repetitions amounting to a realization of "I am nothing," analogous to the fate of the vampires his daughter (Elle Fanning) reads about in her *Twilight* books.

Both movie viewer and star are datum in the grand-scale optics where geographic distance is negated by tele-surveillance. Space is simplified, flattened, and compressed. Banksy graffiti in 2008 announced it's one world "under CCTV," geography laid onto a meta-geography, citizens assuming self-fashioned avatars as players in the new social media empire. Self-expression and communication have evolved, as ideas, while aspiring for the irreverent wit of Banksy, are produced and posted (and reposted indefinitely) as memes, occupying the screen's flat space while lacking the graffiti artist's knack for infiltrating commodified, real space. There's access to more images and information than ever before, but how deeply can we immerse in oceans of accelerating information, brains rewired from concentrated book reading to hyperlink web-surfing? And whose interests and confirmation biases underlie that information in the Virtual Escher echo chamber?

Martin Scorsese's *The Aviator* (2004) is an unlikely progeny of Kubrick, being less a conventional Howard Hughes biopic than a futurist spectacle of engineering, where the engineer (Leonardo DiCaprio) seeks transcendence by collapsing onto his machinery, soaring with transhumanist momentum "above the weather" and creating a new world, though stuck on a mantra before the equipment crashes, "The way of the future. The way of the future . . ." The way of the future is liberating. We can produce our own moving images and publish voluminous blogs; someone is instantly in direct video link with loved ones and strangers across the globe. News feeds are constant. There is ready access to video demonstrations teaching handiwork, fitness, and nutrition. We've reached a kind of psychological time travel contributing to nostalgia's narcotic allure, search tools reuniting us with kindergarten classmates, YouTube granting access to Saturday morning cartoons and advertisements from the past, and myriad entertainment news websites publishing commemorative pieces on motion pictures ranging from the seminal (*Do the Right Thing*) to the tacky (*Troop Beverly Hills* turns 25!). We've mastered the image. Seeing a full-length theatrical movie trailer was once contingent on actually going to a movie theater at the right time and place, whereas now trailers have become their own major event, a matter of immediate access, replay, and speculation, sometimes as much as a year before the advertised film itself is to be released. Viewers can make fan-edits and splice together spoofs of films. The movie's release itself has gradually moved from relying on the here-and-now of theatrical exhibitions to television broadcasts to video access at retailers to pay-per-views to digital discs, finally landing at the disposal of streaming services.

Cyberpunk author William Gibson claims, "The future is here, it's just not evenly distributed." Even in the first world, some people aren't able to afford smart televisions and streaming media boxes. Entertainment and information are reliant on subscription, and so subject to cybernetics (that is to say, who controls the entertainment and information). Disparities in wealth mean disparities in knowledge and a basis of interacting with technology and, given that so much communication is technologically mediated, other people. As Coppola's aforementioned characters disintegrate in the puzzling and privileged ether, Kelly Reichardt's *Old Joy* (2006), *Wendy and Lucy* (2008), *Night Moves* (2014), and *Certain Women* (2016) follow fringe dwellers unable to keep up with the rate of economic and technological change, whereas the stable middle class, with smart TVs, lines of credit, big backyards, and hybrid cars, thrives. Reichardt's marginalized drifters, maladjusted by the stringent-processing conditions of the modern system, dream about participating in an affluent sprawl. How can a progressive idealist lay out real progressive action? Meaningful films, like the Portland-based activist documentaries featured in *Night Moves*, are not enough, as those activist perspectives are dwarfed by surveillance systems registering reality as silent panoptical tedium, the "globalization of the gaze," as Paul Virilio refers to the contemporary state of tele-surveillance.

The Italian neorealists gave the impoverished voices by simply turning their cameras sympathetically to them. Eighty years later, the optics are rampant but nuanced sympathy obfuscated by a purportedly objective "official" buffer. There are more cameras, and so more stringency—and, for privileged people, more safety—but not more clarity. Presently, the publicity surrounding police shootings has led to the planned implementation of body cameras, but even then, with more information stored and disseminated, the reality and truth of a here-and-now moment doesn't seem to be more conclusive, but less so, images picked apart and deconstructed by private interests, filtered through media spin that makes the image, even in its full transparency, more inscrutable. Kathryn Bigelow's *Zero Dark Thirty* (2012) brought the issue of surveillance, violence, and objective history to an embattled intersection of ideas pertaining to the world since September 11, 2001—when it seemed that the society of spectacle went live and never ceased—concluding with the raid on Osama Bin Laden's compound in Pakistan. Though accused of jingoism and endorsing the CIA's torture methods, Bigelow constantly considers the presence behind the viewfinder, its one image of Bin Laden rendered as a camcorder's DV image framing his corpse in close-up, out of focus, and the target's identity riddled with a cloud of uncertainty akin to the morality that dissolved almost immediately following the September 11th attack. The photographic record complicates veracity. As Scorsese said in press junkets in 2010, speaking about *Shutter Island* (a film about mental illness, American history being as ruptured and filled with contradictory narratives as the inner life of Leonardo DiCaprio's embattled, traumatized protagonist), "There's no such thing as a true image anymore."

To see isn't enough in a world of non-stop watchers processing information as if automatically through pattern recognition. Laurie Anderson's *Heart of a Dog* (2015) gorgeously textures film's thick emulsion, the opacity of her meditations—using the framing device of memories of her beloved rat terrier—drawing the viewer away from post-9/11's accelerating surveillance state and toward private, prayerful contemplation. How does what we see affect how we think and feel? Bigelow earlier explored this in her futuristic noir *Strange Days* (1995), where state-of-the-art surveillance tools plug viewers into the recording subject's feelings (for example, excitement during a robbery, or pleasure during sex); banned, this technology thrives on the black market and becomes intrinsic to exposing institutional brutality and corruption. The ostensibly closed system of absolute accomplishment is littered with fractals and ungovernable insurgencies, out of which illuminative, private consolations and grace shine through numbing chrome. In cinema's symphony of gadgets, the dream of reconciling humans to their tools is fundamental.

The impersonal mechanical law translates into our ideals, values, and observations, such as offered by the most famed representative of Hollywood's production factory, Steven Spielberg, whose *Lincoln* (2012) ties the president's storied speechifying and love for narrative to everything from the machinations of legislation to the engineering of a flag pole, the words, once offered, independent of their speaker, to be preserved and contemplated by others, the camera to Abraham Lincoln (Daniel Day-Lewis) having a similar relationship. Spielberg's twenty-first century period output emphasizes the storage space containing images, such as the advanced "mechas" in the epilogue of *A.I. Artificial Intelligence* (2001), the moving pictures and associative feelings received by one of their unearthed ancestors (Haley Joel Osment) sympathetically downloaded to each other through touch, Spielberg himself doubling for these mechas when he engineers an ersatz happy ending—an act of self-deconstruction resulting in a devastating emotional dissonance within the audience. *Minority Report* (2002) entangles us in a sci-fi dystopia of tele-optics so broad that even the future is rendered by oracles as exciting "movie" thrillers feeding our voyeurism, while the past is fetishized and projected as narcotic holograms. *War of the Worlds* and *Munich* (both 2005) jointly dealt with national traumas, the first featuring extraterrestrial optical devices—Dziga Vertov's friendly camera reconfigured as malevolent aggressor—combing through every possible space as the invaders reduce bodies to dust; the latter is a historical thriller where the preponderance of espionage and surveillance shatters the breadth of geographic distance, the site-specific Munich massacre's ramifications affecting the whole world, a unified polis without respite and certainty's comforts, from Munich to New York to Jerusalem to Paris to Tripoli to London.

The digital boom that fell into the new millennium was amplified by the terror and military responses following September 11, 2001, the image, as an abstraction,

dominating our lives and ramping up the question of identity within the information age. Hollywood followed suit,
as after the 9/11 Commission and frustration with the Iraq
invasion around the 2004 presidential election, American
movies genuflected with a national (or this time, global)
malaise akin to the auteurs Kolker studied in *A Cinema of
Loneliness*'s post-Watergate first edition. Coppola, Reichardt, Bigelow, and Spielberg are hardly unique in their
musings of identity in an age of media saturation, total accomplishment of the machine vs. the corporeal reality of
the human body, with recurring motifs of amnesia, screens,
flesh modification, and reckless capitalism.

Paul Greengrass's *United 93* (2006) staged a coordinated terrorist attack with the director's emphasis not on
geopolitics so much as on a mute background of global-
ized modernity, industry, and communications, the drama
of hyperreal information on screens juxtaposed against the
primal and corporeal, the frenzied retaliation of the titular
plane's passengers syncretic with the religious zeal of the
hijackers. As if springboarded from *The Aviator*'s "way
of the future" conclusion, Scorsese's *The Departed* (2006)
enriches Andrew Lau and Andy Mak's Hong Kong thriller
Infernal Affairs (2002) as a Boston cybernoir with allusions
to 9/11 and the Patriot Act, the ethnic gangsters of the director's *Mean Streets*, *Goodfellas*, and *Casino* liquidated as
tribal idiosyncrasies are transferred from inherited cultures
to the anonymity of social security numbers. Similarly
grounded on pulpy material with manufactured identities,
Michael Mann's *Collateral* (2004) and *Miami Vice* (2006)
had digital cameras following a non-stop flow of capital
where identities are manufactured and arbitrary, global
capitalism moving too fast and indifferently for love and
reflection. Alfonso Cuarón's *Children of Men* (2006) imagined a familiar future dystopia plagued by xenophobia,

suspicious terrorism, and mass sterility, art and culture devoid of context and meaning. Tony Gilroy's *Michael Clayton* (2007) and *Duplicity* (2009) considered virtual hyperrealities of realm-and-conquest information wars coexisting with bodily and geographical realities. Richard Kelly's apocalyptic trilogy (*Donnie Darko* [2001], *Southland Tales* [2006], *The Box* [2009]) disrupted suburban nostalgia's warmth with boiling national discontent and post-traumatic stress, geopolitics and pop-culture subsumed in a glossy multimedia death-instinct. Roman Polanski's *The Ghost Writer* (2010) laments post-modern isolation, as the unknowable complexity of historical events is manufactured as tacky narratives, ingested on autopilot by readers. David Cronenberg's *Cosmopolis* (2012) frames capitalist excess as post-human deformation, an uncanny representation of the contemporary world that's curiously in line with the filmmaker's sci-fi body horror. David Fincher examined the evolving nature of cybernetics sprinting toward a Year Zero through his loner anti-heroes of *The Social Network* (2010) and *The Girl With the Dragon Tattoo* (2011), cyborgs rewriting the world around them, their minds melded in perfect coordination with their tools, even their sexuality uploaded into hard drives. And Steven Soderbergh's prodigious post-recession sprint of *The Girlfriend Experience* (2009), *The Informant!* (2009), *Contagion* (2011), *Haywire* (2012), *Magic Mike* (2012), *Side Effects* (2013), *Behind the Candelabra* (2013), *The Knick* (2014–15), *Logan Lucky* (2017), and *Mosaic* (2018) highlights commodified bodies in an accelerating technocapitalist entertainment complex paradigm, corporeal forms corresponding to the filmmaker's conscientiousness—and mastery—of digital film form.

Most of those films are set in the present or recent past, but they are all nevertheless of the future, aspiring to adjust human consciousness to the globaltarian wavelengths of our technology. Even antiquity, like in Oliver Stone's initially neglected and misjudged *Alexander* (2004), reflects concerns with millennial globalization with an inflection similar to his recent hacker biopic *Snowden* (2016), Alexander the Great (Colin Farrell) proclaiming how "we're in new worlds," his sundry Alexandrias with their libraries compressing geography's tangible formidability into a uniform cybernetic accomplishment. And Paul Thomas Anderson's *There Will Be Blood* (2007), set mostly in the early twentieth century, replaces Kubrick's prehistoric humanoids and their bone clubs with the American industrialist using leisure trinkets (a bowling pin in this case) to fulfill the prophecy of the film's title, the industry and possession of oil ensuring there would indeed be bloodshed in the coming century.

The body and memory become vestigial afterthoughts under the hum of industrial ingenuity and growth, their Mephistophelian counterpart in the work of Michael Bay, a far less reputable but no less indelible craftsman whose hilariously—even awesomely—bloated *Transformers* spectacles (2007, 2009, 2011, 2014) put female underwear models on the same plane as automobiles, Bay's filmmaking the fusion of human and machine as the zenith of industrial design. Unlike *The Aviator*'s sterling design that malfunctions in congruence with its subject's mental defects, Bay's *Transformers* series is unburdened by dissonance, his work supercapitalist propaganda of established mores and tastes, and so even better displaying a dystopic "way of the future." Spike Jonze's *Her* (2013) dares to tell a love story between a man (Joaquin Phoenix, in a performance seemingly modeled on Gene Hackman's clever toolman Harry Caul in 1974's *The Conversation*) and his OS (voiced by Scarlett Johansen), the aesthetic of the whole film not unlike a high-tech advertisement of positive feelings, at odds with lingering smog and all-too-human discontent. And

INTRODUCTION: "THE WAY OF THE FUTURE"

Denis Villeneuve's *Blade Runner: 2049* (2017) makes the ambiguities of artificial intelligence in Ridley Scott's 1982 predecessor null and void, suggesting all of its characters are of a simulacrum apparatus, the travails of these artificial beings acting as a measure of the viewer's own capabilities of sympathy and identification.

*

The movie apparatus changed around the time of James Cameron's *Avatar* (2009), and not merely in terms of scale. Our interface became different. The "orga" celluloid images are now the flat transmissions of digital packages. Movies can be viewed on laptop computers and on smart phones. Does the impact change? Do we adapt accordingly to this rate of change? There are celluloid "reactionaries," like Christopher Nolan or Quentin Tarantino opening a new film in 70 mm, but those experiences are pummeled by the demand for fast, big, and all-too-digestible nostalgia tent-poles, Marvel, DC, and the *Star Wars* universes having their slates written up through the beginning of the next decade—studio mandates that the audience demands and craves, full scale movie universes downloaded into each other. The message migrates to other mediums, directors like Soderbergh (*The Knick*, the phone app *Mosaic*) and Louis C.K. (*Louie, Horace and Pete*) experimenting with the possibilities of television and the internet, or Francis Ford Coppola's ongoing "live cinema" *Distant Vision* workshop; there is a by-the-books ESPN documentary (*OJ: Made in America*) unexpectedly emerging as one of the most thorough distillations of troubled American race relations through the last fifty years; a long-form music video opening up the medium's possibilities rather than plainly conforming to fashionable dictates (Beyoncé's *Lemonade*);

and while we may seem estranged from the "real world" by our devices, an app like Pokémon Go turns the entire planet into an interactive scavenger hunt.

While the state of the image and cinema remains fertile, there's legitimate worry about the idiosyncratic artist in Hollywood, indicative in film advertisements where, instead of the "from the director of . . ." tag-line, there's an abundance saying "from the studio that brought you . . . ," a corporate branding in line with the classic studio paradigm, but with the big studio personalities (Jack Warner, Darryl Zanuck, David Selznick, Samuel Goldwyn, Louie B. Mayer) uprooted by zero-sum financial goals. The accelerating rate of buzz and capital means movies have to perform big and quick, its Thursday night sneak-peak grosses—before opening wide the next day—already sculpting a viral box office narrative sealing its destiny as success or failure.

The most critically appreciated film of the new century, David Lynch's *Mulholland Dr.* (2001), casts Hollywood as a merciless and bizarre dreamland of malevolently enforced strictures smothering artistic creativity, focally that of an aspiring actress (Naomi Watts). Lynch's follow-ups, the experimental feature *INLAND EMPIRE* (2006) and the epochal television sequel *Twin Peaks: The Return* (2017), digitally infiltrate the dream world apparatus, apocalyptically dramatizing malleable narratives of wastelands seized by the dread hum of mass surveillance, while paradoxically leaping into the rhapsodic possibilities of the heroic personality (Laura Dern's actress in *INLAND EMPIRE*; Kyle MacLachlan's capaciously receptive and mimetic golem-as-actor Dougie Jones in *Twin Peaks*) transcending imposed boundaries and finding freedom through creative harmony with the digital text in which they exist as performers. Similarly, the star performer (Juliette Binoche) of Oliver Assayas's *The Clouds of Sils Maria* (2015) endures social media's tacky surfaces and affirms herself, the title setting's geographic Nietzschean reference clawing back to Kubrick's *2001*, the actress a conscientious star child before a postmodern audience. All these performers are in a labyrinthine theater of the mind, pendulating from silence to irradiation, the value of art in such metamorphoses. We too are in that theater and in metamorphosis.

This circles back to Dillinger's internal dialogue with the screen in *Public Enemies*, a vital film released at the digital turning point. I can be pragmatic about the future and cinema, but I refrain from enthusiasm for "the possibilities" of the future in lieu of concentrated contemplation. Our gaze on Dillinger's gaze on Myrna Loy is a circular prayer coasting on the wings of engineering and artistry. Dillinger left prison's monochrome walls and reinvented himself through this medium of the gaze and its romance, and now he encounters spectators of his mythology in a movie theater, precipitating his relinquishment of his body. The inscrutable digital ghost-man comes into the light on 35 mm material and is morally vulnerable. He secretly spied his lost horizon on a black-and-white twilight, gently whispering a message to Billie, to be relayed by his assassin (the Texas Ranger Charles Winstead, played by Stephen Lang), preserving him as two-fold public and private myth. The relationship between Dillinger and that emulsion is so intimate that we forget he's at the Biograph on a romantic date with the tragically peripheral Polly Hamilton (Leelee Sobieski), who trembles in a quick medium shot moments after Dillinger is shot before being expunged from history.

This aweing machinery steals away our souls, sometimes poignantly and often cruelly. My aim in this book is to explore *Public Enemies* as an extraordinary accomplishment against a backdrop of other digital films, its meditations on the form precipitating *Blackhat* (2015), Mann's stunning and widely ignored cyberthriller that converts the movie-house celluloid of its predecessor into a beguiling labyrinth of code that's colonized the heretofore tangible firmament right under our noses.

1

2009 AND THE NEW IMAGE

Released to mixed reviews and middling box office success in July of 2009, Michael Mann's *Public Enemies* is retrospectively one of the most curious and significant films in cinema's migration from analog to digital. Mann pioneered HD cinematography in the mainstream with *Collateral* (2004) and *Miami Vice* (2006), building on the new technology aesthetically and grounding its use on practical photographic utility. In *Public Enemies*, this hyperkinetic video approach within a 1930s-period frame troubled many critics and viewers. Set on an impressionistic canvas following American outlaws in flight from encroaching law officers, *Public Enemies* is a great filmmaker's bold big-budget experiment of film—or video—form, its reflexive formalism harmonizing history in a strange new sound, aspiring to conjoin the mythos of John Dillinger (played by Johnny Depp) with politics and culture, history and celebrity, filmmaking and film-watching, all in the gorgeous matrix of a spellbinding new age.

Public Enemies emerged at a cinematic fulcrum point. Filmmakers had made the leap from analog to digital some time before, Mann experimenting at the forefront with a few scenes in *Ali* (2001) and then more comprehensively in his short-lived Los Angeles TV show *Robbery Homicide Division* (2002), which served as a sort of small-screen demo for the widescreen canvases of *Collateral* and *Miami Vice*, the former winning several year-end awards for its cinematography. While other technophile directors like George Lucas, David Fincher, Francis Ford Coppola, and Steven Soderbergh advanced their aesthetic on this new template, Mann's distinctly idiosyncratic use of HD cameras rattled viewers with its alien video-ness, explicating to viewers that they were perched on a separate filmic architecture that may require a new way of seeing. Branching off from a new visual apparatus was a different modulation of not only editing and sound, but also Mann's increasingly paratactic approach to his characters, as their detailed backstories, while provided by the director to his actors during pre-production, diminished textually as the bodies in his digital frame were lassoed into the shackling grid of binary data *as* data, vaporous existences and stories struggling to materialize in an accelerating cyberspace vacuum. His artistry expresses a paradox of visceral sensory verisimilitude that tilts toward—without wholly embracing—baffling avant-garde pure cinema abstraction feeling aesthetically closer to David Lynch (*INLAND EMPIRE*), Albert Serra (*Honor de Cavelleria*), Jean-Luc Godard (*Film Socialisme*, *In Praise of Love*), and Abbas Kiarostami (*ABC Africa*, *Ten*, *Shirin*) than other big studio digital filmmakers. His films tacitly prompt a formal dialogue where style generates substance, while the final products are still part of the big studio mass-cult entertainment machine. The resulting films are replete with earnest sociopolitical and spiritual inquiries. *Public Enemies* projects the future into the past, and poses questions concomitant with the arguments and speculations about film, politics, and human beings that were part of an urgent philosophical movement.[1]

Public Enemies was released before digital had usurped 35 mm projection booths in theaters[2] and the exhibitive delivery package would change over, kicking longtime projectionists and their flickering equipment out of theaters. It was also just a few months before the paradigm would perhaps undergo its most significant popular shift with the release of James Cameron's *Avatar*. Cameron used the digital tools to create a fanciful Edenic hyperfirmament, a collision of the real and virtual. *Avatar* was a $500 million gamble that sparked a revolution, ensuring

---

1. Mann compares his use of DV to approaches in architecture, as when steel was introduced it was made to appear like old masonry. "It wasn't until Louis Sullivan's pioneering work in Chicago in the 1890s that the aesthetics of the steel structure were allowed to be expressed" (Olsen, "Paint It Black."). In 2012, Peter Jackson's experimentation of 48 frames-per-second 3-D in *The Hobbit: An Unexpected Journey* prompted a response from critic Ignatiy Vishnevetsky that Jackson's problem was that the new technology had little to do with the movement within the frame, as if Jackson was still playing by 24 fps rules. Vishnevetsky cites Pedro Costa's *Colossal Youth* (2006), "which makes deliberate use of MiniDV's slightly ghostly sense of movement in its wild grain"; Mann's *Public Enemies*, "where every shot presents a different sense of motion"; and Lynch's *INLAND EMPIRE*, "which mines the blurry, bleary motion of consumer-grade video for oneiric effects" as counterexamples. "Not one of these films moves or looks like 24-frames-per-second film is supposed to; *The Hobbit* looks conservative in comparison—and that's precisely the root of its problem." Vishnevetsky, "What Is the 21st Century?"

2. Speaking with *Village Voice* critic Bilge Ebiri at the Brooklyn Academy of Music on February 12, 2016, Mann cited the conversion of digital data files to cheap 35 mm prints as a reason for some audiences reacting negatively to the look of *Public Enemies*. He stresses that his digital films—*Collateral, Miami Vice, Public Enemies, Blackhat*—should all be theatrically projected as DCPs, digital cinema packages.

that most blockbuster releases would have 3-D exhibition, signaling that the possibilities of this new world, *Avatar's* planet Pandora doubling for the future of cinema, were limitless. With the real-world tactility of *Public Enemies* and the full-on graphic design of *Avatar*, Mann and Cameron could be seen as the new cinema's juxtaposed figureheads, speculating how the image is changing and how we change along with it, their dual approaches incorporating in one case the historical mythos of master criminal and folk hero John Dillinger, and in the other an archetypal myth framework building on extraterrestrial imagination. Both films are about private, hidden lives eluding the hampering systematic control of a surveilling panopticon, the audience's interaction part of the experience: we reflect onto John Dillinger seeing himself and Billie Frechette in a gangster melodrama at a movie theater, and we double for *Avatar's* paraplegic protagonist, Jake Sully (Sam Worthington), who escapes into a pixelated 3-D alien planet.[3]

3. While his aesthetic approach is different from James Cameron's, Michael Mann admired *Avatar* so much that in 2012 he listed it, alongside the likes of *Apocalypse Now*, *Raging Bull*, *Battleship Potemkin*, and *The Passion of Joan of Arc*, as one of the ten best films of all time for the British Film Institute's annual poll (http://www. bfi.org.uk/films-tv-people/sightandsoundpoll2012/voter/1069). He comments, "Upon the foundation of an entirely invented biosystem, *Avatar* is a brilliant synthesis of mythic tropes, with debts to Lévi-Strauss and Frazier's *The Golden Bough*. It soars because, simply, it stones and transports you." Admirers of Mann may be baffled by his hyperbolic love for *Avatar*, and I will approach this problem in this book's section on *Blackhat*, suggesting that *Avatar* enervated Mann, so influenced by Dziga Vertov and the Kinoks, as something of a monumental utopian digital manifesto on the evolving film form.

2009 And The New Image

*

Avatar's futurism resonated in 2009 with its wounded war vet protagonist, environmental concern, and references to gaming and social media. But *Public Enemies'* aesthetic conjoins the quandaries of contemporary cyberspace and globalization with the cultural problems of its 1930s setting, a time when philosophers were concerned about the power film had over the public, as burgeoning political ideologies vied for control of nations.

Central to that discussion was Walter Benjamin's landmark essay, "The Work of Art in the Age of Mechanical Reproduction," which tells us that cinema is necessarily bereft of the "aura" of other arts. Subject to photographic replication, motion pictures were distributed across the globe in thousands of prints, unspooling several times a day and consumed as frivolous escape for audiences, who would have a substantially different interaction with them than an ancient Greek would have with a sculpture. Ancient art would often have a cultic, religious role to play. There is also the question of utility and aesthetics, such as with architecture. Photography changed so much because the optics of the camera were so different from the human eye, and so a photographic replication of a painting would essentially be a different encounter from seeing something unmediated in a here-and-now context. The movies could meanwhile liquidate history through propaganda and be a great tool in subduing and controlling masses of people.

The Frankfurt philosophers, with whom Benjamin was associated, were Marxist Jewish intellectuals from Germany, alert to how the government used media to control populations. Fascism aestheticizes politics, the viewer not "clobbered into submission," as Benjamin puts it, but appeased into a volitional submission, which, as Kolker says in his analysis of Benjamin, typically connects "out of the most profound and uninformed aspects of a culture's collective fears and desires," and "confirmed and reinforced the basest instincts of that culture."[4]

Even the most well-intentioned films are thus problematic as products of this apparatus. *Public Enemies* was mass-produced art, shot and edited digitally, distributed to thousands of multiplex movie theaters, and starring two big-name movie stars (Johnny Depp and Christian Bale). Yet it's conscientious of how media semiotics affect and control people, simultaneously expressing the human need for freedom. It's a theme familiar to Mann, whose *The Insider* (1999) opens with Lowell Bergman (Al Pacino), a mass media (CBS's *60 Minutes*) journalist who we learn idolizes Frankfurt philosopher Herbert Marcuse, blindfolded in Beirut. The first image is Bergman's point-of-view, an extreme close-up on stuttering cloth. The director controls what we see and there are ramifications to how we process images. How does a big budget film hold onto its integrity in the Hollywood apparatus? Or a journalist at a major network? Or an audience member working a 9-5 job, dependent on an income and insurance? In each case, the subject compromises out of necessity, yet treads a thin line. *The Insider* and Mann's subsequent feature *Ali* (2001) are about men threatened by images imposed on them, and who in retaliation work to subvert those images, subjective individualization working against insurmountable and imperial zero-sum axioms.

In *Public Enemies*, John Dillinger interacts with mass-art. He's a romantic, projecting himself into that media through the force of his imagination and scripting a romance with himself in the lead role, his spirit commingling with Billie Holiday's voice on the radio and Clark Gable's

4. Kolker, *Film, Form, and Culture*, 70–71.

countenance at the cinema. Many people have a powerless, automatic response to the media they encounter. Benjamin writes of the possibility of the viewer having an active, intimate dialogue with the art. He writes, "The progressive reaction is characterized by the direct, intimate fusion of visual and emotional enjoyment with the orientation of the expert."[5] Unfortunately, critical engagement is less likely in a mass consumable like a movie, where the audience at large can dictate one, individual reaction. How is the viewer activated instead of ossified? Can John Dillinger, and we, truly have that intimate dialogue with this mass-market, replicated product?

Contemporaneous with Benjamin was the intellectually enlivening dialectical cinema sense postulated by early Soviet filmmakers, such as Sergei Eisenstein and Dziga Vertov, cited by Mann as being two of his primary influences.[6] There's a dynamic mechanism to art that affects the viewer, rooted in formal engineering, the same way a poem gets its charm from the construction of meter and accents of vocabulary, or in painting how the eye follows one element which creates an impression, which then collides with a second element in the painting; in cinema, the filmmaker uses the elements of image (including shape and

5. Benjamin, *Illuminations*, 234.

6. In F. X. Feeney's beautifully arranged book Mann says of his influences, "Stanley Kubrick, Eisenstein, Vertov and Kino-Eye; I mean that's really my aspiration. So my approach to films tends to be structural, formal, abstract and humanist" (*Michael Mann*, 100). A superficial critical approach to Mann can confuse such a formalist as an empty stylist. In the same book Mann says, "I don't like style. Style is what happens when form is orphaned because content left; it's good in commercials. My attitude is that the audience is a highly sensitized organism sitting there in a dark room and everything has an effect" (54).

spatial relationships) and montage.[7] Cinema's technological ingenuity is not empty mechanics working to soothe us as docile machines, but has the potential to reach into hearts and minds, affecting change through dialectical methods of thinking (and, for the Soviet theorists, revolution, as workers of the world are united by *seeing*)—a new way of thinking and seeing the world outside of the theater. The camera eye may not only be imitating the human sensory process, but, as Vertov saw it, it was independent from it, capturing something we couldn't see. How are our sensory and intellectual processes evolving in imitation to the camera and montage? Can a cinematic method enliven us and enrich life, beyond entertaining us and serving as an escapist portal? Mann is one of many filmmakers walking the tightrope of popular entertainment and personal expression, administrating over immense productions with complete control. Watching his films we struggle with the problem of reconciling the agent of mass production in a capitalist economy and romantic notions of the auteur.

Those creative idiosyncrasies, out of sync with the bulk of movies in whatever genre (action, biopic, historical), have provoked some industry analysts to wonder why he is still allowed to wield such power.[8] That his unparalleled technique and vision has endured for so long is a glowing affirmation of how art works in the mainstream. As an

7. This is an oversimplification of what the Soviet theorists, who were in contention with each other, wrote and practiced, and while we see their influence, not merely formally but intellectually, in directors like Michael Mann and Terrence Malick, their differences in regards to what later generations have rejected are just as striking. In addition to the films of Eisenstein and Vertov, their writings are commended, particularly Eisenstein's *Film Form*, and Vertov's *Kino-Eye*.

8. See Friedman, "*Miami Vice* Theme"; Masters, "Hurricane Michael"; Masters, "Knives Out for Michael Mann"; and Lawson, "Will *Public Enemies* Be Just Another Hollow Michael Mann Movie?"

information age filmmaker, he considers serious Frankfurt School questions regarding the digital curriculum, where the speed of life sprints toward paralyzing seizure. How does the individual remain grounded and hold onto integrity in such a hyperreal, evanescent—vast with information and yet too fast to plum much depth—landscape?

Public Enemies is terse, showing off its mechanical wiring in its design while off-setting the humanistic conventions that hypnotize Hollywood audiences. Its extraterrestrial suturing is paradoxically immersive and detaching for the viewer. The director's eye for detail brings us in closer intimacy with the blooming romance of Dillinger and Billie than with other romances, just as the heightened apex of Elliot Goldenthal's music score syncs into the characters' emotional rhythms sewn by Hollywood melodrama. Their inner lives are partial constructions of the growing cinematic world of the early 1930s, shortly after the movies began to talk; in the case of John Dillinger, who was released from a monochromatic decade-long prison sentence that began in the early 1920s, the early talkies were supplementary elements acclimating him to a society that had leapt into modernism since last he saw it.

As a filmmaker whose form generates content, Mann's challenge is having us feel what Dillinger feels, putting us in dialogue with a motion picture that's questioning our responses to this unfamiliar sensate and syntax. In Dillinger's world the *movies*, after all, are progenitors to a new mythology, constructing and then verifying our everyday self-presentation and making sense out of human experience in terms of relationships, loves, deaths, much as Dillinger experiences cinema (specifically *Manhattan Melodrama*) in a mediation that's both profound and prosaic, just moments before his last stand. The cinematic construction of the self for Dillinger is circularly reinforced, his image of identification (Clark Gable) being a Hollywood adaptation of the myth Dillinger himself conceived through the mediation of movies to begin with.

In *Public Enemies'* opening minutes there is the leitmotif of enslaved movement through a given vector: a chain-gang marching; Red Hamilton (Jason Clarke), masquerading as a law official, shoves hand-cuffed Dillinger toward a prison gate; Walter Dietrich (James Russo) limps through work area columns. The movement is geared toward opening and passing through blocked entrances (which will be more excitedly demonstrated during the mid-film Crown Point jail breakout, where Dillinger must get through *eight* doors with a fake gun). The motif is analogue to the whole movie, which is wound up, set on the ground with the title placard "1933," and then driven forward to a final, inevitable destination.

This theme has been constitutive of Mann for decades. In *Thief* (1981), Frank (James Caan) criticizes Jessie (Tuesday Weld), the woman he's courting but who is hesitant to quit her diner job and couple with him: "You're marking time is what you are. You're backing out, you're holding out. You're waiting for a bus that you hope never comes, because you don't want to get on it anyway, because you don't want to go anywhere." In *Heat* (1995), bank robber Neil McCauley (Robert De Niro) is associated with movement and direction (think of the street arrow over which he walks at the film's beginning), though his oceanic final destination isn't realistic. In the famous café scene opposite his rival, cop Vincent Hanna (Al Pacino), he relays a recurring dream: "I have one where I'm drowning and I have to wake myself up, otherwise I'll die in my sleep." "You know what that's about?" Hanna asks. "Yeah," McCauley replies, "having enough time." In *Collateral* (2004), taxi driver Max (Jamie Foxx) is driving in circles across Los Angeles with big dreams but with little resourcefulness to realize them: he's been driving a cab for twelve years while building up the impractical business plan for a limousine company (Island Limos), lying to his mother (Irma Hall) about his success, and even when an attractive and successful passenger, Annie (Jada Pinkett-Smith), gives him her number, it's unlikely he'll muster the gumption to call. His next passenger, sociopathic hit-man Vincent (Tom Cruise) taunts him with the truth: "'Someday? Someday my dream will come?' One night you'll wake up and you'll discover it never happened. It's all turned around on you. It never will. Suddenly, you are old. Didn't happen, and it never will because you were never going to do it anyway. You'll push it into memory, then zone out in your Barcalounger being hypnotized by daytime TV for the rest of your life." *Manhunter* (1986), *Heat*, and *Miami Vice* (2006) all contain a memorable Mann mantra: "Time is luck." We can't negotiate with gravity, Sonny Crockett (Colin Farrell) says to Isabella (Gong Li). Time is moving quickly and with each succeeding film it moves faster and more unsteadily, Mann's more austere tripod and Steadicam compositions—tools that outline and caress the tactility of a time and place, aspiring to make it permanent in a painterly frame—are replaced by a nervous hand-held camera, while the world is de-aestheticized with panoptical tele-surveillance: time won't stand still, and any time one has is divested of privacy, a theme central to *Public Enemies* with its portrayal of the beginnings of a national surveillance network where the "enemies"—and all citizens, perhaps—are "public" data.

"Time is luck." In *Public Enemies*, Mann goes back to his hometown of Chicago and the small Wisconsin towns surrounding his alma mater in Madison, where on a freezing winter night, as a young literature student, he first saw G. W. Pabst's *The Joyless Street* (1925) and walked home resolved to become a filmmaker. In 2009, his art form was undergoing an inexorable paradigm shift. Change (like death) is inevitable and sudden, and the men in Mann's films flee from determinism while struggling to catch up and preserve themselves in the sensate thrill of right now. Much like an artist in his autumn years—or celluloid in the twenty-first century—these characters are running out of time and their eyes thirstily venture and fix on the *image*, some picture, some expressive moment with an intimation of everlasting warmth and calm. Where are these characters going? But what more, as Mann's characters reach out through the gulf of their tactile corporeal physicality to soulfully transmigrate into the flickering communicative power of pictures, where is the cinema, and the image, going?

The real self is nonexistent, ghostly, and the only place John Dillinger can be captured and killed is under the blinking lights of a movie theater, because he's more real there, by this temple of images, than anywhere else. *Public Enemies* wonders about the historicized self and how that self dissipates within evolving cybernetic systems. Using Frankfurt School vernacular, the state becomes realized as an idea of absolute control and reason, and people within that Right Hegelian system created and personified by J. Edgar Hoover (Billy Crudup), such as the tragically alienated Melvin Purvis (Christian Bale), are consigned to withering stuffed shirts and animated limbs, slowly dying and forgotten, hollowed out by pernicious alienation. Just as *Public Enemies* separated itself from other summer blockbusters (it opened opposite Michael Bay's first *Transformers* sequel), or even—if not especially—"realistic" (which is to say, familiarly lavish and elegant 35 mm) period films, Dillinger is an individual of unique conscientiousness. He is alone with the myths, determinedly reaching through the suffusing signal-to-noise for the sublime monad. *Public Enemies* similarly reaches for aura as diverse idiosyncrasies are muffled and flattened by the acceleration of technology and art under the auspices of global capitalism. It is a pearl of digital cinema. The startling DV form of *Public Enemies* entangles the subject (viewer) with the object (film), prompting a consideration of whether we absorb the film or it absorbs us. The form perfectly suits the themes. It is a film about John Dillinger, but just as centrally, *it is a film about experiencing films*.

2

LAST OF THE FRONTIER FOLK HEROES

The criminals described in Mann's source material, Bryan Burrough's book *Public Enemies*, are different from the organized crime figures of the twentieth century's underworld mythology. Their distinction is that they are the outsiders. John Dillinger, Alvin Karpis, Baby Face Nelson, the Barkers, Machine Gun Kelly, Pretty Boy Floyd, Bonnie Parker, and Clyde Barrow were all famous within a specific time frame beginning in the 1920s and ending with Karpis's arrest in 1936. To say that they became bank robbers because of the Depression is not wholly accurate given that bank robbery was budding beforehand. According to Burrough, the reason bank robbery became a viable "career" option for lower-middle class middle-American individuals had much more to do with technology, specifically the machine gun and the development of V-8 automobile engines. These tools were widely available, and when expertly used they ensured that someone could out-gun and out-run the otherwise disorganized local police officials, who were themselves susceptible to bribery, the greatest example being the fiduciary relationship between the police and criminals in St. Paul, Minnesota, an infamous safe haven.[1]

Dubbed by J. Edgar Hoover as the "public enemies," Dillinger, Floyd, Nelson, etc. represent a breed apart from the popular syndicate figures dramatized in films like *The Godfather* (1972), *Goodfellas* (1990), *Bugsy* (1991), *Casino* (1995), *Donnie Brasco* (1997), *The Departed* (2006), and *Black Mass* (2015), or the ethnic tribes that developed into highly structured organizations, run by names like Charlie Luciano, Frank Costello, Meyer Lansky, Benjamin Siegel, Mickey Cohen, and Al Capone. This anthropological structure carried something commensurate with ageless secret societies, the dynamics of their gang hierarchies, rites of passage, inner conspiracies, and back-stabbings (literal and metaphorical, often both) carried the lofty weight of courtly drama, such as John Gotti's assassination of Paul Castellano in midtown Manhattan, the mystery of Jimmy Hoffa's murder, or Kevin Weeks taking the witness stand against James "Whitey" Bulger. Most of these figures also had ties—even by blood relation—to legitimate political figures.

By comparison to this regal opera, the "public enemies" were anarchic proletarian street theater. They were not part of an organization; they were committing crimes because it was the one thing at which they had much skill, and having begun it and being catalogued in the system as offenders, there was no way out for them. Though many of these characters, like Nelson and Barrow, were sociopathic, testimony indicates that others, particularly Floyd, were aware of their social bind and poignantly envious of the people they robbed. They wanted a normal life with a stable

1. See Maccabee's *John Dillinger Slept Here*, which served as a favored collection of source material for Burrough.

family, a house with a room of their own, an idyll where they could be comfortable and free.[2]

A man like Luciano, on the other hand, was not a public enemy: he didn't really live among the public. The syndicate gangsters were contained within a huge corporate body that made it somewhat reflective of the courts of law in the United States. Although the syndicate was responsible for more terror, murder, and illegality than the public enemies of the Midwest, the fact that it had a stable apparatus, "structure," made it less of a threat. Hoover, an aesthete obsessed with structure, appearance, and organization, didn't acknowledge them. Nor did they carry the sway of the public's imagination the way the public enemies did. The satanic is a Romantic image, but the cabal isn't. Milton's Satan found admiration from the Romantics because he was a poetic rendering of an individual absurdly going up against an implacable hegemon.

In America's literary mythology, with prophets like Walt Whitman and Mark Twain, the mythos is hummed in a pitch of the Romantic and pragmatic, the narrative of a dually ancient and virgin frontier colliding with

---

2. A depressed Floyd reportedly said to Sheriff Jack Killingworth, whom he was holding captive, "There's no turning back for me now. . . . Too many policemen want me. I haven't got a chance except to fight it out. I don't aim to let anybody take me alive. . . . I might not have been this way, you know, but for the damned police. I might be going straight, be living with a family and working for a living. I finally decided, you're determined I'm a tough guy, a bank robber, that's what I'll be. They have themselves to thank. . . . How would you like to be hunted night and day, day and night? How would you like to sleep every night with this [submachine gun] across your knees? . . . I have a son, too. Maybe you think I wouldn't like to see him. When you get home, you can have your son with you every day and sit and talk with him. All I ever get to do is see mine once in a long while. Then all I can do is stand off and look at him for a minute" (Burrough, *Public Enemies*, 45).

civilization's burgeoning machinery and factions fighting for control. The vast frontier is an abstraction with transcendental reference, offering promise that will always be fulfilled in time, never "now," but always in the future. It is the New Jerusalem toward which we wander in the wilderness, and for much longer than forty years. The freshness of American geography during the nineteenth century made its literature contrast to England's Romanticism, where there is already melancholy and aching futility, the abbeys and castles having infested the countryside for centuries, death rattling in its desire to control timeless spaces; human passion is reduced to hauntings, like *Wuthering Heights'* mourning ghosts. But the possibilities in the American mythos are infinite and incalculable where life and death, as in *Leaves of Grass*, are part of a false binary, our architectural columns and creeds subsets in a cosmic poem we can read through the wind and trees over fertile soil.

English Romanticism is beset with something Ecclesiastical, where hope and striving are destined for disappointment. That the English countryside had been conquered many times since the Roman Empire reminds one of the present's fallibility. America in the 1850s, when Whitman published the first edition of *Leaves of Grass*, was still unfinished, fragmented, with sundry mysterious paths into the dark woods awaiting discovery. "History," that accounting of time, hadn't yet arrived. There was apocalyptic expectation for the future, which to this day infects American consciousness in its eschatological strands of Christianity.

The American "Event Horizon" continued from Whitman and Twain to the modernists with the emergence of Hemingway, Faulkner, Steinbeck, and Fitzgerald. The frontier had been conquered with agriculture, and the drive for money had subsumed the contemplation of nature. The frontier had turned inside out, ever-present in

American consciousness though passing into a sacred no-where. American modernism's Don Quixote is Jay Gatsby, who with his capital gains dreams of acquiring something virtual, unreal, the green light always out of reach. Time's gravity is a prominent theme in this melancholy literature, where Fitzgerald's heroes are deluged by history and the frontier no longer belonged to humanity or nature but, as Steinbeck writes, now belonged to a strange, impersonal consciousness controlled by the flow of capital, the bank, which was the state, the corporation, or whatever hege-monic force shackling the continent. Emerson's Over-Soul, where every organism is connected, was reduced to a dust-bowl wasteland plowed by lonely machines driving families from domiciles. The remaining vestige of the frontier lay in "California," the paradise the Joad family moves toward in *The Grapes of Wrath*. The transcendental cushion of eter-nity is replaced by a sense of fatalism carried forth in the paratactic sentences of Hemingway. Death is curt, swift, and final.[3]

The public enemies are interesting in this historical context because of how *public* they were. And though the public were besieged by the brutal realities of the Great De-pression, advancing technologies allowed them to spectate in the theatre of recorded history: radio and talking mov-ies gave life a prism where real world experiences could be

3. In his DVD commentary for *Public Enemies*, Mann mentions Hemingway's book on matadors, *Death in the Afternoon*, and how the book's fatalism mirrors how the public enemies lived their lives. Mann's directorial style in his late digital period, curt and paratactic, is stylistically congruent with Hemingway. In the 2000s, Mann was developing an adaptation of Hemingway's 1940 novel *For Whom the Bell Tolls*, interestingly alongside a film about Robert Capa, famous for his photographs of the Spanish Civil War. The theme of death captured by the camera, preserving the liminal existential boundary, corresponds to Mann's sensibilities and themes as the photographic medium evolves, especially in relation to *Public Enemies*.

given an immediately digested context and meaning, in addition to escape and, per Walter Benjamin's ideas, a way for power structures to wield control over the people. Myths were transmitted and projected, and the movie theater was an air-conditioned democratizing temple replacing the bonfire. Heroes and gods were given the concrete faces of Fairbanks, Pickford, Muni, Dietrich, Gable, Garbo, Grant, Hepburn, Flynn, and Cagney: a freshly projected ideal, a final frontier and undiscovered country, a new religion.

More significant than the organized criminals controlling neighborhoods and huge events (such power rigging the World Series, as Arnold Rothstein did in 1919) were the criminals presented to the public. They were romantic figures representing freedom from the constraints keeping people poor and immobile. They were paupers who had fooled the system so that they could sneak into the castle and live like princes, but never held silent by the elitist *omertà* oath. And being in the public, they were witness to their own metamorphosis into romantic figures, in turn manipulating their images and even influencing each other. For example, in his bid for a public relations makeover, Clyde Barrow told a bank customer to keep his money because he was there "for the bank's money," something he had appropriated from the printed stories about Dillinger. Dillinger's robberies were performances where he would live up to his stage reputation by putting his coat on a hostage to keep her warm, and being warmly jovial with bank customers—despite his capacity for virulence.

John Dillinger is an important part of this American mythology, and even as a criminal his mythology is not really morally suspect, unlike Bonnie and Clyde (whose grandiose, sentimental mythology was almost wholly created by Arthur Penn's 1967 film) or the fictional Corleones in Francis Ford Coppola's *Godfather* trilogy (1972, 1974,

1990). Dillinger represents the rugged frontier individual struggling to maintain freedom in a place where freedom doesn't exist anymore. Born in rural Indiana and always on the road, Dillinger's association with freedom is nature's fecundity, as opposed to the banks he robbed and the law-men pursuing him who, despite the efforts of Hoover and Washington, would always be representative of the imper-sonal machine working against the public, a divide put into Woody Guthrie's "Ballad of Pretty Boy Floyd": "Yes, as through this world I've wandered / I've seen lots of funny men / Some will rob you with a six-gun / And some with a fountain pen / And as through your life you travel / Yes, as through your life you roam / You won't never see an outlaw / Drive a family from their home."

Dillinger is a hero with no definitive political or ideo-logical association, his drive for freedom through stretches of frontier space appealing to both leftists and libertarians. This land is our land, no single entity should own it, and a phenomenological experience of it brings one back to an incendiary Ground Conception of this land that is more powerful than the rational, control-bent Hegelian systems leading to history's finality. John Dillinger was a Great Depression Christ (he had more charisma as a leading man than the similarly "martyred" Floyd), and even at his 1934 trial his lawyer, Louis Piquett, invoked this by stating "Christ had a fairer trial!" Representing a spirit at such odds with the system's cold mechanics, when the country is in-creasingly industrial with political leaders inextricably tied to big business and capital interests, Dillinger was a pre-ternatural force that the system couldn't contain, slipping through its bars and wires, performing escapes that played like miracles. Imprisoned, he could free himself like a wild element, battling a system that only protected and served the interests of power, not the individual and his family.

But John Dillinger was not poor. Born in a well-off middle class family during a time when the middle class scarcely existed, he was a ne'er-do-well youth. He exhibited little ambition. His mother died when he was three and he had a troubled relationship with his father, from whom he was never able to get approval. He longed for a justification but lacked the skill to acquire it. His problem was an inability to settle down. His drive to escape imprisonment was displayed in his failure to hold down a job, a marriage, or military service, as he went AWOL *twice* in the Navy. He had the yearning to go somewhere but no plan, which furthered the strenuous relationship with his father. His inability to settle coupled with how he always ended up back home manifests a paradox of constant escape and a need for domestic warmth.[4] Dillinger wanted to flee Mooresville, Indiana, but only so that he could return. He was a variation of Gatsby, falling forth into time so as to grasp the time he had lost in the past, perhaps related to the maternal love he was missing. His luck turned for the worse after getting drunk and robbing a local grocer of $550. He was sentenced to fourteen years in prison. He emerged from nine years in Indiana State Penitentiary as the consummate bank robber. He had been "baptized" by the older and more experienced inmates he befriended, composited in *Public Enemies'* Walter Dietrich, their methods derived from Herman K. Lamm who had developed a rigorous bank-robbery curriculum influenced by a background in the Prussian military, such as the "casing" of banks and the importance of "gits," or getaway maps. Dillinger would hone his craft to such an extent that he awed those he robbed. News headlines sealed his myth, full of stories both popularly eye-witnessed and apocryphal.

4. Burrough, *Public Enemies*, 136–37.

As Dillinger's legend grew, the world condensed. More advanced surveillance systems and communications were instituted so that reality could no longer be apocryphal. The myths would be projected and televised, machinery dictating its course and influence. Aura was lost and so was the potency of folk symbols. Dillinger and the public enemies' demise was perhaps the last gasp of the folk hero. The frontier was conquered. Reality was officially "official," as J. Edgar Hoover ushered in an imperial interstate hegemonic all-seeing matrix on what was, once upon a time, the New World.

3

MECHANICAL EYES, TACTILE BODIES

Mann's film is an elegiac chronicle of the last American folklore myth, simultaneously fastening the archetypes to the deft urgency of his cameras that mediate a feeling of presentness. But contrary to the elegiac, it doesn't feel like any other historical epic. Like its predecessor *Miami Vice*, its structure is built on pursuit and escape as if the film was trying to catch up with itself, as Hoover—and history—tries to catch up with Dillinger. It is not a nostalgic historical representation but a self-reflexive suggestion of our twenty-first century media-sculpted historical consciousness, which was yet of great concern in the 1930s. Time and space are manipulated by historical conclusion in the service of the Hegelian God (Hegel being considered the first cybertician) and the science of the machine. *Public Enemies* is frustrating in its denial of respite, and yet poetic and poignant when interpreted by the active viewer that sees the archetypes in cinema as projections of private, inward experiences.

Mann's method of presenting this world to us with cameras that call attention to their presence reinforces a need for exegesis. We have never seen a period film like this before. Our ideas of the period world—and costume period *film*—are inverted. Mann believes that cinema is a consensual dream, an extension of consciousness, and he dares take us away from our preconceived notions of the time as elegantly rendered in *The Untouchables* (1987), *Bugsy* (1991), *The Road to Perdition* (2002), or more recently on its digital canvas, *The Curious Case of Benjamin Button* (2008). On release, a recurring question of reviewers and audiences had to do with the relevance of its errant optical approach and why we should care about such a story being presented as it is. "Why?" asks Richard Corliss in his *Time* magazine review.[1]

According to Jean-Baptiste Thoret, *Miami Vice* was a new kind of espionage film mirroring 24-hour news cycles and global immersion into video images and surveillance.[2] The binary codes surrounding one's life and work are more important that one's thoughts and experiences. Freedom is constricted by a social security number, the cipher for identities.[3] It is not our recession anger toward AIG and the

---

1. Corliss, "Kill Dill." See also a camera industry insider's disdain for Mann's choices at Luzi, "Top 5 Directors."

2. See Thoret's excellent essay "Gravity of the Flux," and his overview of Mann in his book *Talk About Cinema*, 228–29.

3. That Mann and Scorsese, two directors often grouped together because of their violent work (unfortunately categorized as "masculine"), would release remarkable films on this theme in 2006 is highly interesting, particularly given Mann's switch to digital and Scorsese's devotion to 35 mm. Crockett and Tubbs (Colin Farrell and Jamie Foxx) are integrated into this future system, sometimes looking back, but numbly moving forth with their fabricated identities and work; their story in *Miami Vice* moves like data, in sync with its form. *The Departed*'s hero, Billy Costigan (Leonardo DiCaprio), works undercover but is troubled by conscientiousness of his origins and

big banks that made John Dillinger's story relevant to its release date, but rather the growing dependency on virtual systems hindering one's ability to find "a room of one's own" (offline, anyway). All time, Mann is arguing, is present, and yet always pulled forth by temporal gravity. Cinema's presentation of history is linked to how technology sculpts that fragmented chaos. What the film is showing us—and what we experience everyday through camera phones—is not a human perspective but the ingenious construction of machines, corresponding to Vertov's ideas put forth shortly before *Public Enemies*' setting and so connecting to the psychology of the period Mann is dramatizing: "The machine makes us ashamed of man's inability to control himself, but what are we to do if electricity's unerring ways are more exciting to us than the disorderly haste of active men and the corrupting inertia of passive one. . . . I am kino-eye, I am a mechanical eye. I, a machine, show you the world as only I can see it."[4] In his appreciative video essay defending *Public Enemies*, Scout Tafoya notes how Mann's grammatical understanding of the new media startled audiences with its immediacy in capturing flesh and movement. "It looked uncomfortably close to us," he says. Tafoya points out how Mann hit on a new cinema sensation working from the awareness of how digital images were now "our dominant mode of expression," from personal cellphones to the stars of reality television.[5]

Our biological optical abilities are not the same as a camera's, but the language of film that has surrounded us

---

background, and is resolute to hold onto it, while his nemesis Colin Sullivan (Matt Damon) eagerly dissolves into systematic duplicities. Fittingly, when Sullivan is killed, Scorsese doesn't allow his blood to splatter the tidy, Ikea-decorated white walls of his trendy apartment.

4. Vertov, *Kino-Eye*, 7, 17.

5. Tafoya, "Unloved, Part Thirteen."

for the last century confuses this, and the visuals of movie drama become our own drama, filtering into our memory and being edited, scored, constantly reedited, and then up for critical reevaluation. Identities are remolded by technology, and so is history. This is romantic and problematic, heightening subjective memories and yet making objective reality vulnerable to everything from totalitarian propaganda to reality TV fashion-frenzied tackiness, the romance of the cinema screen fractured and drifting toward total virtualization, surveillance, coercion, and exploitation. Walter Benjamin theorized how fascism aesthetizes politics in the 1930s, just as Hoover does with his public enemy newsreels at the same time, and just as political candidates like Donald Trump build their base from reality TV stardom in the present.

Public Enemies hurls us into a time and context and after sending us into orbit makes us rely on our cognition to do the work. "1933" the film's opening title says, much like the beginning of Mann's *The Last of the Mohicans*, which opened with "1757" and then threw us into an *in medias res* elk hunt. "It is the fourth year of the Great Depression. For John Dillinger, Baby Face Nelson, and Alvin Karpis it is the golden age of bank robbery." The first images are set within an institution with great vertical lines of imprisonment behind chain gangs marching in formation. "Indiana State Penitentiary—Michigan City, Indiana." That is all the information we are going to get. Incepted, history will now begin moving and there will be no non-diegetic material to assist us: no backstory, no prologue, no narration, no more titles. We are moving forth in time like the inmates are walking in determinate lines, a visual motif throughout the film. The prison establishes a rhythm based on contrasts: muted and muffled sounds with sharp loud ones; large establishing shots with precise rack-focused close-ups evoking the intimacy of Carl Theodore Dreyer and Robert Bresson; wide spaces and closed-in space; the deep blue sky and clouds with the dwarfing prison architecture. The visual language is so immediate and tactile through its mesh of objects and movement that we cannot lull in it. We may be mesmerized by what we see but we can't dwell in it with relaxed passivity. Accommodating two-shots or medium-shots with pristine dialogue or conventional shot-reverse-shots are eschewed. Smoothness is practically nonexistent in favor of the corner-jutting confines of hand-held images. This is a film that does not want to be contained anymore than a prison inmate with a lust for life.

Cutting to outside the prison walls we see a black car pulling up. Two men in dark coats exit, one of them wearing a badge, the other with his hands cuffed. The badged official shoves the prisoner ahead, the camera slowly tracking with them from a distance. The steel doors open. At another location in the prison, the camera follows veteran inmate Walter Dietrich, close on his face as he carries a box. We can discern information from this close-up. His face suggests he is inured by prison life, a circumspect thinker, and his experience verified by a limp. He lays the box down by another inmate, Homer Van Meter (Stephen Dorff), and from the box they pull out two guns. Their escape is precisely coordinated, Dietrich and Van Meter soon accompanied by portly Charles Mackley (Christian Stolte), stick-figure Pete Pierpont (David Wenham), and clumsy Ed Shouse (Michael Vieau). This group overpowers the unsuspecting guards and leaves the inmate work area.

Meanwhile, the guards recognize the new prisoner as a recent parolee, John Dillinger. "You didn't last long," he's told. Quickly, the handcuffs fly off Dillinger's wrists and he points a machine gun, forcing the other guards to open the cell-door. The ostensible lawman pulls out a shotgun; this is John "Red" Hamilton, who makes his way back outside to prepare the car (his exit outside, so muted and held in a long-shot, is a marked difference from the hard, close angles of steel and panic happening within). Dietrich's group meets Dillinger and swap their inmate garb with the guards' clothes. Abrupt and unexpected violence, owed to Shouse's incompetence, triggers the prison alarm, and the group hurries to exit, the subsequent gunfire like a drizzle that quickly becomes a torrential downpour, a few spattered gunshots turning into a violent staccato of fired weapons, fallen bodies, and shattered glass. The fugitives move toward the car but Dietrich, physically the weakest link in this shaky exodus, is mortally wounded by a long-range rifle from above. He clasps Dillinger's hand as the getaway begins.

Mann shoots both men in shot-reverse-shot medium close-ups. Dietrich seems to smile at his protégé while pulled along with the car, his eyes emptying of life. The emerging source music, "The Lagoon" from Hans Zimmer's score for Terrence Malick's *The Thin Red Line* (1998), isn't at all propulsive, but rather contemplative: bodies in motion, stumbling toward their final destination. Dillinger looks into Walter's dying eyes and is forced to let go of his mentor, the inert body's velocity braking to zero on its fatal vector as the car accelerates onward, a victim on the Hegelian slaughter bench in a moment that likely quotes a similar film about the law—and mortality—closing in on a criminal on the run, Carol Reed's *Odd Man Out*.[6] Mann is

6. While Mann in interviews seems evasive about the question of other films influencing his work, *Odd Man Out* feels distinctly like a close blood relative to *Public Enemies* as much as other crime films feel distant from it. Reed, like Mann, follows a sympathetic fugitive (James Mason) whose legend takes an active hold on the public. Dying from a gunshot wound, the fugitive drifts through the Belfast night almost like a ghost, inhabiting life and death simultaneously.

interested in this grave philosophical conflict of individual freedom vs. absolute freedom, found in citizenship and service to the status quo. Dillinger's gaze into the dying man's eyes, a recurring motif throughout *Public Enemies*, relates to the quest to preserve life, dreams, and memories, as visibly tactile substance flickers out and disappears into nothingness, the slaughter bench of history without meaning or actualization, "drifting into the night," as Dillinger later says. The intertextual nod to *The Thin Red Line* doesn't feel arbitrary, given the Malick World War II film's recurrence of Private Witt (Jim Caviezel) looking, as if optically *searching*, into the eyes of the dying, grasping for permanence within war's merciless meat grinder. But the platoon has to head through the hills and the getaway car keeps on moving. Can John Dillinger embrace "letting go"?

Is his individuality a Hegelian triumph, being that this picture is about the "becoming" of his own mythology in the larger culture? The subjective John Dillinger will come to realize the importance of this sociological construct, "John Dillinger." It is this which affirms his love and legacy, giving hope to masses of people in dark times, much how Mann frames his previous biopic *Ali*, when Muhammad Ali (Will Smith) encounters street murals depicting himself as a hero for the poor people of Zaire.[7] Mann's historical

The hold of both the law and the criminal organization (modeled on the IRA) are subterfuges to the ideals of Mason and his lover (Kathleen Ryan). For both filmmakers, death seems to be the only guarantor of freedom. Composer Elliot Goldenthal's mournful *Public Enemies* score even seems to have major themes modeled on William Alwyn's highly regarded music for *Odd Man Out*.

7. Mann portrays Dillinger, like his Ali, as a genius semiotician understanding how what he says and how he looks says something. "Dillinger was an avid reader of his own press clippings, and no one suspects this penchant for niceties had less to do with good manners than with an increasing awareness of his own public image" (Burrough, *Public Enemies*, 165).

protagonists, Dillinger, Ali, and Howard Hughes, though molded by their times, have no desire to become a part of the state as civilians under the established conformity of law. They want to hold on to their subjectivity and beliefs (Ali wants to be the peoples' champion, but he will use that power of influence in a way to satisfy a worldview far different from how Joe Louis was the peoples' champion), but contingency complicates the goal and injures the communicative vehicle, the mortal body. Ali *has* to beat George Foreman in Zaire because of the tacit sociopolitical message underlying the fight, but his physicality is past its prime, the "tools" aren't what they used to be. There's collusion between the body and mind and camera, affecting us as the miracle is on mass display, the body's image changing hearts and minds as it is read.[8] Dillinger's body is read in relation to his momentum through space. He is always on the run, trying to master the infinitely changeable variables. "How far away's the farm?" he asks, referring to a safe house. "3.2 miles," Hamilton answers, indicating this relationship with time and space is so important that it be regarded in specific increments, like the timing of a bank robbery. Clocks and maps become significant props and set decorations in *Public Enemies*. They must be mastered and perfectly coordinated with literal time and geography for survival.

8. See Schwartz, "Body and Soul," and Ebiri, "Now Is the Time." Mann's overlooked biopic doesn't differentiate its formal qualities as a motion picture from the mechanics of training and using the body, both of which, while reducible to material weight that wears with time, hold great, transcendent power in their ability to express eternal themes and palpably move spectators. Ebiri and I wrote our pieces soon after Ali's death in 2016, and while his body had been debilitated and muted by Parkinson's disease for decades, it's arguable that few other bodies had as much cultural impact over the last fifty years.

Mann cuts to a low angle of Dillinger, looking from west to east, the camera tracking alongside him as he scans the horizon. This is the empty frontier of immense space that he will use as his maze while robbing banks and fleeing to safe houses through the Midwest. The image, reverberating something romantic and religious, suggests something incalculable that cannot be contained by time and technology. It's scored to a spiritual, "Guide Me O Thou Great Jehovah" by the Indian Bottom Association of Old Regular Baptists, referencing a distinct American dynamic. It's Native American and tied to the geography of the ageless frontier, while suggesting something biblical and that this individual quest will be a religious journey toward spiritual apotheosis, John Dillinger's "Becoming." Germane to a film focusing on individuals caught between determinism and freedom, Old Regular Baptists are known for having split into factions, one favoring absolute Calvinist predestination, and the other absolute free will. Interpreting *Public Enemies* is troubling because it has theological and philosophical precepts that are rife with contradictions.

The action is quickly stitched together. Coming to a safe house, the men wrap food up in newspaper, their dialogue muffled. Instead of luxuriating in the moment, Dillinger and company—like the film—are rushed. The camera follows them leaving from inside, stopping close to the wall where we see the conspicuous erosion given to stillness. Outside the house, the woman living there stops Dillinger. "Take me with you, Mister," she says, and the camera slows down. "I can't, I'm sorry," Dillinger replies, and the camera continues moving at its original tempo, Dillinger outpacing it, the woman, holding her child's hand, growing smaller and the house and drying bed sheets blowing in the wind. It's a powerful, melancholy image and to linger on it longer would have made this an even more lush (more comfortably "period") film, but *Public Enemies*, like its subject, is restless with the necessities of plot (history) outrunning our desire for solace and permanent beauty.

This is an approach that Mann had also utilized in *Miami Vice*. It complements both films' narrative structures of momentum, which give cause for audiences to be unbalanced as the films may come across as uneven and a little jarring. Steven Rybin commented on *Miami Vice* in his essential book-length study on Mann, saying that the film captures "an immense depth of field in certain shots that renders the world . . . as simply overwhelming, too much to experience visually in a single viewing of the film. At certain points while watching the film during its initial theatrical release I myself felt an acute desire to hold onto individual film frames for longer than Mann was willing to let them linger on the screen."[9] People are pushed forth through time, always in the present on a set course, as Calvin's God always sees people in His linear universe of predestination; they do not have a personal historical context or hope for future plans. Underlying the deception of this static beauty is the fact that time still moves and that the house, if we remember the walls, is eroding. The woman here is held down by her socially imposed domestic responsibilities as house-body and mother, seeing the flight to the wilderness as a gate to freedom. But it is impractical, expressed as we see the child tugging at her hand. Her encasement in the past feels much like Walter Dietrich's demise, another slaughter-bench victim.

9. Rybin, *Cinema of Michael Mann*, 205.

4

"OUR TYPE CANNOT GET THE JOB DONE"

Consonant with the intimations of fate expressed during the Dillinger Gang's flight from Indiana, Mann verbalizes the passage of helpless bodies through time musically by using Otis Taylor's bluesy banjo song "10 Million Slaves," the lyrics telling how modern everyday labor, repeating itself day after day, is analogous to slaves crossing the ocean with shackles on their legs. History never changes, only appearances do: "Don't know where, where they're going / Don't know where, where they've been," is repeated over and over, indicating a constant "presentness," individuals having no history or future, and the final destination is always solitude: "Sun goes down / You'll be standing / You'll be standing by yourself." The song also expresses the film's difficult narrative method to an audience accustomed to elaborate exposition where the plot and characters can be cleanly surveyed so we can calmly make sense out of everything, relaxing as we sit back and are lulled into docility.

The film, with its Calvinist God-like mechanical eye, doesn't care about the characters' past. It's interested in where they are *right now*. The two characters introduced during the song are predator and prey heading down a linear vector: an apple orchard, where nature has been conquered and groomed in such a way to make a deterministic straight line through which a man in a bright blue suit, Pretty Boy Floyd (Channing Tatum), runs from a rustically groomed lawman calmly aiming his rifle, Melvin Purvis.

The camera runs with Floyd as he flees, the light-weight HD image startling, even surreal.[1] Purvis aims and fires, blowing a hole through Floyd's midsection. Dying, Floyd insists his name is "Charles Floyd," as if he's trying to set free his factual biological identity in front of his *socially* given one as an outlaw. His determined running and unwillingness to be subdued even when clearly beaten (he pulls out a revolver while on the ground, which is quickly kicked away by Purvis), indicates that any kind of entrapment is to be resisted. He is a cornered animal clawing for freedom. This sequence abstracts the relationship of the individual's need to freely establish his own identity as the larger system implants its staple on him. Yet this is not an either/or being that the reference to "slaves" without a past and future here is ironic, as we'll observe in Purvis. Floyd rebels against the system's shackles as Dillinger does, but Purvis, the bona fide FBI man, is a slave without a past or a future, inextricably tied to his job and image.

Critics and audiences have complained about Mann and Bale's collaborative characterization of Purvis. In his

1. Floyd has actually come quite far. In reality, Pretty Boy Floyd was killed soon *after* John Dillinger. Mann and his screenwriting collaborators Ann Biderman and Ronan Bennett handily adjust historical timelines to establish Purvis, but, whether deliberate or not, the practical screenwriting maneuver rather charmingly fits with the film's themes of the inability to be free from fate and state control.

introduction to Tafoya's video defense of *Public Enemies*, critic Matt Zoller Seitz—while a fan of the film—addresses this as the film's weakest aspect, comparing the character and performance to how Mann handled pursuant lawmen in *Heat*, fronted by Al Pacino's Vincent Hanna. "Part of the problem is Bale's acting, which consists mainly of variations on tight-sphinctered righteousness, but to be fair, he isn't given much to work with," Seitz writes. "His Purvis might be the least fascinating lead male character in Mann's entire filmography. . . . There's not much for a viewer to latch onto it."[2]

Purvis certainly lacks exposition and the time to reflect on his quandary, but reading in-between the lines of Bale's performance, there is a tremendous portrayal of stifling despair and base submission to a system at odds with a good man's natural disposition and upbringing. Purvis is deliberately antipodal to the venerable lawmen of Mann's past movies. *Heat*'s Vincent Hanna, according to Mann's DVD commentary, is one of the only two self-aware people in the world of *Heat* (De Niro's Neil McCauley is, naturally, the other), carrying his angst with him while chasing his prey. Purvis is a good man but, given his compromise of conscientiousness to act the part given to him by his "director," J. Edgar Hoover, he's tragically self-alienated, and Bale's grasp of Purvis's impotence is one of Mann's most devastating accomplishments.

While Purvis answers the press's questions later on, we see him putting on a movie star affectation. Factually, Hoover—and the media—liked Purvis precisely because he resembled Clark Gable and had a movie-star look.[3]

2. See Seitz's editor's note on Tafoya's video essay in Seitz, "Unloved, Part Thirteen."

3. "Hoover ribbed Purvis that a newspaper's description of him made him sound suited for Hollywood: 'I don't see how the movies

Vincent Hanna (and Crockett and Tubbs for that matter) is also much better at his job. Mann may be a few steps ahead of his critics through the big-star counterpart set-up—Dillinger vs. Purvis, Depp vs. Bale, Captain Jack vs. Batman—and then laying out the trick where Dillinger's true counterpart is the tacit, decisive Texas lawman Charles Winstead, who's no performer. Purvis, historically and as dramatically rendered here, was a competent lawman but he botched several attempts to capture Dillinger and the public enemies. The strictly mechanical regiment of Hoover's Bureau kept agents in a lock-step binary mindset, where they were separated from the people they pursued. On the other hand, Vincent Hanna and *Manhunter*'s Will Graham (William Petersen) not only use forensics to capture their prey, but psychologically identify with them. "All I am is what I'm going after," Hanna admits. Purvis is not as introspective. *Public Enemies* dramatizes our encounter with images, and for Dillinger the reflective image leads to something dialogical; Purvis is also embodying an image but, as when he encounters Dillinger in jail, the steel bar covers his mouth as he speaks. There is no dialogue, only dominance and utility.

Mann cuts away from the restless Midwest action and "10 Million Slaves" to Washington DC, where J. Edgar Hoover is questioned by a congressional panel. Hoover is looking for more funds to establish his revolutionary Bureau, introducing "federal" law enforcement that can bypass corrupt and fragmented local jurisdictions while aiming to pursue, capture, and kill the public enemies running rampant and robbing banks. A federal system is needed, Hoover says, and his architecture for this system, the FBI,

---

could miss a "slender, blond-haired, brown-eyed gentleman." All power to the Clark Gable of the service'" (Burrough, *Public Enemies*, 65).

will embody the spirit of what he believes is historically essential, ushering in the modern. It excludes idiosyncrasy, not only geographically, where locality is overridden by the federal structure, but the private idiosyncrasies of individuals, whose work environment is a clockwork mechanical structure where even the aesthetic is based on utility. In Hoover's FBI, an agent could be fired for being a minute late, and one's desk was a replica of all surrounding desks; personal photographs or mementos were not allowed. Hoover's vision of the FBI was a bureaucracy of college-educated men, an amalgamation of law enforcement and an office, scientific and logical deduction being more valued than street experience and intuition. The dapper Hoover disdained "rough-looking" individuals not interested in strict office protocol. He wanted his agents to be a social emblem for bourgeois respectability without any kind of disarming individual quirks. They were stuffed suits with ties, their notepads more important than guns.

In *Public Enemies*, Hoover's screen time amounts to a little more than five minutes, but his power is the feature that drives the narrative toward the future, where the federal grid is clasped around the nation and freedom is smothered. The film's structure, where characters are disallowed historical context ("don't know where they're going, don't know where they've been" sung as Pretty Boy Floyd runs to his final destination) corresponds to Hoover's "modern age." His opening scene, where he is arraigned harshly by Senator McKellar (Ed Bruce), establishes with brilliant economy his motives, character, and threat. His fortuitous ascension represents the cancerous growth of an American fascism, shadowing events in Europe. As Hoover explains how his Bureau has been successful, McKellar stops him. "How many criminals have you apprehended, Mr. Hoover?" Hoover claims that the Bureau has apprehended a large number of criminals, validating his success. "No, I mean *you*, Mr. Hoover. How many have *you* personally arrested?" Hoover is stifled. "I have never arrested anybody." He is less of a human being than an institutional cyborg, an abstraction with jowls handing down facts and figures but unable to relay the grit of tangible experiences when dealing with lawlessness. "I am an administrator," he says. Hoover is espoused to mechanical functionality, disdaining the human element of interactive work dependent on tangential intuition.

McKellar pursues his agenda opprobriously. "I think you're a front," insinuating that Hoover is running wild with control as he implements an expansive system capable of wielding more power than law-makers. Even if such a system as the Bureau were to gain a desired position of legitimacy, McKellar says, "I wonder, Mr. Hoover, if you're the kind of man fit to run it." Hoover is indeed a "front," a new kind of modern being of virtual dynamism owed to his publicist, Harry Suydam (Geoffrey Cantor), who has powerful ties to the print media. Systems are administered by individuals, but when that individual is more devoted to implementing a system of control instead of basic service and protection, the morality of governance is vulnerable and suspect. Hoover wants to consolidate power, taming the wild frontier of erratic local law (and individualized) jurisdiction, pursuing a cosmological dominance over the unpredictable atomic particles of quantum mechanics. As Hoover leaves the room, Mann's camera tilts beneath his heavy countenance and peers at a ceiling painting of uniformed men on tamed horses, an image repeated later on, relating a dominion over nature.

Validating what McKellar alleges, Hoover tells Suydam to contact Walter Winchell, feeding information that "McKellar is a Neanderthal," a subhuman (and inconsequential) hinderer to progress and modern ideals. "We'll fight them on the front page," Hoover says. The dialectic toward the "truth" has been lost to the constructs of power and public control bought with propaganda in mass communications. "Reality" is not in the context of the argument, but in the printed or recorded information that is manipulated by institutional hands, projected onto an easily controlled public. We see this method of automated media control later, when Dillinger and his pals watch newsreels. Hoover's method of relating to the rest of the world is tacit, *subliminal*, registered by the camera fixing on Hoover's longtime companion (and alleged lover), Clyde Tolson (Chandler Williams), who quietly surveys as Hoover speaks. Tolson's apparent narrative inconsequence is contradicted by the camera, which establishes him as ubiquitous and ineffable, an embodiment and extension of Hoover's modern system that does not use language to communicate. It doesn't need language. It has no dialogue. It sees and controls.

Cut to Purvis sitting in front of Hoover's office. Groomed perfectly, Purvis looks like an office fixture rather than a nuanced lawman. The two walk past the replica desks, Hoover informing Purvis that his objective will be to capture John Dillinger, "public enemy number one." Outside the federal offices, Hoover stops in front of sundry assembled reporters (again, Mann's economy and utility in storytelling is itself worthy of Hoover) and declares, "The United States of America's first War on Crime," directly casting Melvin Purvis in the role of the special agent that will capture Dillinger. The one-dimensional presentation is what matters for Hoover, and that feeling extends from himself to Purvis, who raises an eyebrow (like Clark Gable) and answers how he captured Pretty Boy Floyd. "Through an apple orchard," he says with graceful poise.

Purvis names the tools he will be using to catch Dillinger, who lacks such advantages. "The Bureau's *modern scientific* techniques," and "the visionary leadership of our director, J. Edgar Hoover." This scene may seem relevant to a twenty-first century audience given that Hoover's tactics were similar to how the CIA pursued the War on Terror following September 11, 2001 (the impetus for Hoover and the United States government was a combination of the "Kansas City Massacre," where federal agents were brutally killed while escorting an arrested criminal, in addition to Hoover's need to keep his job, jeopardized by the election of Franklin D. Roosevelt; he needed to create a successful program that would be publicized through media and cement his reputation; Hoover was, as McKellar claims, a "front"). This reinforces a binary about the corporate hegemon's technology, where everything can be extrapolated, deduced, and controlled, versus untamed natural elements, as in a previous scene we saw Dillinger's gang disappearing from an urban bank robbery into the forest. Purvis, his directive handed to him and modus operandi established, becomes like the (theoretically) cyborg cop in Ridley Scott's *Blade Runner* (1982), who doesn't know he's a cyborg, in pursuit of other lawless replicants. He is inextricably tied to his job's technical apparatus.

Dillinger is also part of this new apparatus, being that Mann's focus during and after a bank robbery were the technology and functional dynamics allowing the Dillinger gang to accomplish their goals. The bank robbers are part of a larger organism: Dillinger gets the safe open, Pierpont and Mackley cover the interior ground, Van Meter stays outside and watches the door, Hamilton—his eyes on a clock—waits in a getaway car with an escape route on the dash. Their new submachine guns are more advanced than the weaponry the police have. They have faster cars. They rely on the proficiency of engineers, and at a safe house we see a gunsmith retooling a weapon's structural problems, while some "real fast cars" are shown off for sale outside. When Dillinger escapes from Crown Point jail, he asks the garage mechanic for the best car and is directed to the one that has the new V-8 engine.

The difference between Dillinger and Purvis is that one is using technology to achieve his own ends while the other's job and personality is blurred within the very paradigm of a technology synonymous with modernity. Speculating on analogies between the War on Terror and the War on Crime, there is a contrast between human intelligence versus the technological intelligence acquired by surveillance. The bodies caught within these wars, when it is purely based on the technological, become inconsequential materials. This becomes a problem for Purvis, who is repeatedly associated with a simulacrum of civilized constructs, versus Dillinger, associated with nature and a frontier extended outward over the horizon and inward toward imagination and dreams. When Mann shoots both characters with his HD cameras, Purvis's backdrop is often arrays of windows from a building next door, while Dillinger has the open sky and empty space of an Edward Hopper painting.[4] Even the car carrying Dillinger is painted with trees reflecting on its surface as it flees into the forest.

In Dillinger's world, where technology and human beings flow more easily together, the human relationships are friendlier, even between opposite sides of the law, opposite sexes, and different races. While the gang reconstructs itself at the safe house, Dillinger has a friendly conversation with Chicago police chief Martin Zarkovitch (John Michael

---

4. The Art Institute of Chicago featured an Edward Hopper exhibition in early 2008. Mann says he visited it frequently for research during *Public Enemies'* pre-production.

Bolger), who says that Dillinger will be safe in the city. With them is a friendly Romanian immigrant, Ana Sage (Branka Katic), a brothel madame running her business in the city. "Come and visit the girls," she says to Dillinger. There's harmony here, given that exchanges are as symbolic as they are material. Dillinger robs banks, pays off salesmen and engineers for tools, and robs more banks. He pays off Zarkovich out of generosity, not because he has to—it's after Zarkovich tells Dillinger he's safe in Chicago when Dillinger offers "a little something" in an envelope. It's a gift, not a payment. Zarkovich also protects Sage's prostitution ring, which offers sexual intimacy to Dillinger's gang (and, we can presume, policemen), and so is also funded by the bank robbery boom. None of these relations are abraded by a sense of obligation or control, but are rendered as active exchanges between respectful individuals working within their own niches and sharing the fruits of their labor with each other. Its corporeal structure is basic, with different organs cooperating while sustaining themselves independently.

Compare this to the two big corporations in the film that aim to consolidate power, the Federal Bureau of Investigation and the criminal syndicate, one fronted by administrator J. Edgar Hoover, the other by Chicago boss Frank Nitti (Bill Camp), whom Mann also develops as someone not-quite-human. Dillinger himself comments that Nitti "looks like a barber"; this man, probably one of the most powerful in the country, is devoted to endless growth rather than leisure, and as played by Camp, Nitti never seems to be enjoying himself (in this sense he then relates to Mann's globally networked cartel leaders in *Miami Vice*, rarely smiling with all their wealth, as they sit and watch Bloomberg TV and hatch future plans). In Miami, Nitti says to his top assistant Phil Deandre (John Ortiz), "It's hot, right?"

"Yeah, Frank." "Since those pricks shot me I can't get warm." Frank Nitti is just as much estranged from his biology—that which ties him to other human beings—as Hoover. He wields enormous mechanisms of impersonal control, but is unable to be a real person. Mann treats his antagonists quite unusually, choosing to emphasize the spirit of something uncanny and strange, whether it's Hoover's apparent pathology, Tolson's ghostly gaze, or the bizarrely subhuman Nitti.[5]

Dillinger runs and the world changes. On a radio, a newsman reports that Dillinger "roams the wild" while federal agents pursue him, and then notes how the USSR has been allowed into the League of Nations, conveying a less fragmented globe. Mann highlights the uniformity of the modern age by focusing on Purvis's scientific strategy of mechanical deduction: Dillinger gave a coat to a hostage. He was *somewhere*. It was *cold*. He bought a coat. Where did he buy the coat? He was in a safe haven somewhere. "Such methods will help us find him." Mann cuts to one of the film's most striking set designs, a surveillance center where Purvis and his associate Carter Baum (Rory Cochrane) can

5. The idea and imagery of the cyborg in Mann's work, reduced to utility in law enforcement (Crockett and Tubbs, Purvis, the DoJ team of *Blackhat*) or something attributing a sub/post-human appearance (like the cartel kingpin Montoya in *Miami Vice*, Hoover and Nitti in *Public Enemies*, and even Howard Hughes in *The Aviator*) has interesting precedence in cyberpunk author William Gibson's novel *Count Zero* (1987), which for years Mann was going to adapt. Among the main characters are the mercenary Turner, hired by corporations to "extract" information from other corporations (the corporate struggle to control information similar to *The Insider*, which Mann chose to direct instead of *Count Zero*, retitled *The Zen Differential*, in 1998), and Virek, an invalid tycoon whose ethos leads another character to observe, "with an instinctive mammalian certainty, that the exceedingly rich were no longer even remotely human" (Gibson, *Count Zero*, 16). The new sci-fi corporate mode of existence does not espouse individualization.

overhear conversations through any phone line in the nation. The space is limited yet full of global, future implications, appearing like a science fiction planetarium where expansive spaces across the country are compacted to light bulbs held together by wires. In this room, space and time are efficiently compressed to serve the new cybernetic architecture, suggested by one of the few dissolves used in the picture, where a shot of the surveillance room dissolves into another angle of the same room, with no indication of passing time. This is the heart of the machine where time has no meaning, and bodies are recorded and processed.

Purvis explains to his agents, all of whom are basically desk workers, that they will be carrying firearms and dealing with "hardened killers." The abstraction doesn't register in the real world, however. A significant problem in Hoover's FBI had to do with white-collar college grads more attuned to abstractions of law enforcement than to concrete hands-on pursuit and detainment, where their bodies were in danger. Most of these agents lacked experience in strategic thinking and were clumsy with guns. This disparity will prove, repeatedly, detrimental. The nervous agents don't communicate well with each other. When Purvis and his men prepare to enter a hotel where they suspect Dillinger is hiding out, he has to slowly spell out his question, "Are they aware that we are here?" He goes in with another agent to confront a suspicious guest and are cordially greeted by a woman and her fiancé, both providing identification. It's a front, and Purvis realizes it. The genial man is Baby Face Nelson (Stephen Graham), acting the part of legitimate shoe salesman, pointing out that he recognizes Purvis from popular media.

Purvis bids them good night and, once outside, instructs his agent to "stay right here" until reinforcements arrive. Then the lack of the Bureau's human coordination unfurls, totally different from the clockwork function of the Dillinger gang. The surveilling agent moves back into the hotel hallway and is distracted when a suspicious man exits a nearby elevator. The agent awkwardly says, "Bureau of Investigation, what's your name?" The man, Tommy Carroll (Spencer Garrett), remarks as if this adversary was reading from the wrong script, "You wanna know my name?" Nelson then emerges from his doorway and shoots the agent multiple times.

Alarmed by the gunfire, Purvis hurries back and finds his agent near death. Like Dillinger to Dietrich, he stares intimately at the dying man and then runs to Nelson's room. Nelson and Carroll have already left, their getaway car hurrying through narrow city streets. Purvis discovers that the Bureau car, parked so as to block escaping vehicles, has been driven up to the hotel "because we heard gunfire." Purvis is open-mouthed in disbelief. These men are incompetent in the arena against this sanguinary kind of rival.

Disappointed in his star, Hoover chides Purvis. The Bureau has suffered a casualty, Baby Face Nelson has escaped, and John Dillinger has robbed another bank. The crimes, gunfire, and bloodshed are of less interest to Hoover than the negative publicity. Purvis then voices his taboo request. He wants the Bureau to recruit older and more experienced lawmen from Texas, precisely the opposite of what the bureaucratic Hoover wants in his brainchild. "I thought you knew what I was building here," Hoover says, agitated. Purvis's response is unwelcome: "Our type cannot get the job done." What follows is eerie. As Tolson looks on, Hoover petulantly says, "I'm sorry, I cannot hear you." Purvis repeats himself, louder. "I'm sorry, I cannot hear you," Hoover says again, and again Purvis, "Our type cannot get the job done." Purvis's ineffectuality and humiliation offsets our expectations. A chivalrous and handsome lawman—played by Christopher Nolan's Batman—is being put through a behaviorist's conditioning hoop, reduced to a dog being tamed and satisfying the pathological demands of his master.

Leading these Texas agents is the aforementioned Winstead, whose weathered and austere countenance pierces the chrome and steel of Chicago's Union Station. These men have rough, tan visages and wear boots instead of dress shoes. They are antithetical to Hoover's agents, physically and practically. Their real-world devices of intuition forecast how bodies will move in space. Whether Purvis listens to him or not, Winstead will confidently predict how Dillinger moves out of Little Bohemia and later, out of Chicago's Biograph Theatre. When the Bureau finds out that Dillinger is seeing a movie on his last night, Purvis sets up teams at both local Chicago movie houses. Winstead sees a waste of resources. "What's playin'?" he asks. He's told a Shirley Temple movie at one theater, a gangster film at the other. "John Dillinger ain't going to no Shirley Temple movie," he says, lighting a cigarette. Purvis doesn't take Winstead's advice at Little Bohemia, and in Chicago he'll still deploy agents to both theaters. The reputation and protocol of the system discounts human intuition and resourcefulness. Eluding the spotlight of 1930s modernism, the frontiersman ethos of Winstead materializes as Dillinger's foil and conscientious double, the Vincent Hanna to the bank robber's Neil McCauley, not Melvin Purvis.

Dillinger is captured in Arizona, albeit not by the Bureau but by local law enforcement. Up to this point, there's been a consistent smoothness to Dillinger's movement through the country. It's shattered with the law breaking down the door, interrupting a playfully erotic moment between Billie and John. Characters that we were just beginning to get comfortable with, Pierpoint and Mackley, disappear completely, as they will be sent to Ohio for trial, imprisonment, and execution. In his own holding cell, reading a *True Detective* magazine, Dillinger finally meets Purvis, who visits for a sense of closure. It's a brief confrontation that did not in fact ever occur (John Dillinger didn't even become Public Enemy Number One, or of much concern to Hoover and the FBI, until long after his Arizona arrest), but it firmly reinforces ideas and motifs in the film. Both men are already celebrities ("Here's the man who killed Pretty Boy Floyd," Dillinger says as Purvis comes to the bars) with reputations sealed in media headlines. Mann's framing of the conversation is important, as the shot-reverse-shots have the bars obscuring either their eyes or mouths. The discourse here is performative, not dialogical, though Dillinger reaches out on the subject of death. "It's the eyes, ain't it," he says, binding together their recent experiences with comrades dying. "They look at you right before they go. And then they just pass away into the night."

Purvis rejects any symbiotic connection to Dillinger. "Goodbye, Mr. Dillinger." "See you down the road," Dillinger says, unable to close off their relationship. "No you will not," Purvis says declaratively, the bars covering his mouth. He is a different kind of prisoner. "The only time we'll see each other again is when we take you out to execute you." Purvis walks away an apparent victor in terms of who lives and who dies, but Dillinger throws a verbal dagger. "Better get a new line of work, Melvin." Bale dramatically pauses hearing that utterance, framed in one of Mann and Dante Spinotti's beautiful close-ups, the HD eating away Purvis's visage. He's been hurt. Though Dillinger was caught, Purvis failed, and also feels much less alive than his subdued adversary, existing as a citizen and ward of the state and not a subject unto himself. His identity is dissolving. He can't speak, he can't *be*.[6]

6. The important theme in Mann's work of dialogue's decay is thoroughly explored in Wildermuth's illuminating study *Blood in the Moonlight: Michael Mann and Information Age Cinema*. The framing of Purvis and the bars in his one exchange with Dillinger is consistent with the duplicitous, power-determined dialogues in his films, where, really, "there is no discussion," as Leo says to Frank in *Thief*, the heretofore avuncular boss threatening his recalcitrant employee's life and family. Dialogue is one-sided and power-driven, complicating relationships corporate (Jeffrey Wigand's gag orders and threatening emails telling him to "shut the fuck up"), political (Muhammad Ali and the US government in *Ali*), and domestic (Vincent and Justine rarely look at each other while talking, their initial argument bearing a telling set decoration of a painting—by one of Mann's daughters—with a woman's eyes closed and mouth covered; later Neil doesn't talk with Eady so much as he expects her to listen to him). *Manhunter* complicates this, almost poignantly even, with Dollarhyde's tormented pathology, his expressive weapon (he leaves vampiric bite marks on his victims, courtesy of prosthetic teeth with fangs) repressed in duplicitous romance with Reba—their lovemaking scored to Shriekback's "This Big Hush," and concluding with him using her sleeping hand to cover his mouth as he weeps; he's a psychotic prisoner to impulses that deny exchange and demand monological dominance. Yet in contrast to this is the climax of *The Last of the Mohicans*, when colonial soldier (and jealous lover) Duncan (Steve Waddington) undergoes a fundamental reversal when he has to actively *translate* the English of Hawkeye (Daniel Day-Lewis) into French for the Huron. Only in that active translation, demanding that he listen and be empathetic to what's being offered in conversation, does he finally understand the complicated socioeconomic dynamics involved in the French-Indian War, offering unexpected sympathy—and ultimately sacrifice—for characters he assumed the privilege to control and dominate until now. CBS producer Lowell Bergman in *The Insider* and Muhammad Ali in *Ali* exhibit a talent for communicating ideas, inciting their spectators to listen with engagement, and possibly being a source for positive social change.

5

EMBODYING ROMANCE

In Chicago's Aragon Ballroom, the issues of temporal plans are addressed when Dillinger meets with Alvin Karpis (Giovanni Ribisi). Karpis asks if Dillinger wants in on a plan to kidnap a rich St. Paul banker, Ed Bremer, which, given the success of a similar kidnapping months before (the Hamm Brewery kidnapping, also in Minnesota), would be lucrative for everyone involved. "I don't like kidnapping," Dillinger says. "Why not?" "The public doesn't like kidnapping." "Who cares what the public thinks?" "I do. I hide out among them."

Dillinger is conscious of the identity he is creating and how he is mediated to the public. Just as Hoover wants to control reality through mass communications, so does Dillinger. To become a kidnapper means that he would be a home invader, something disdained by Mann's heroes in other films because it violates the sanctity of the family and privacy. Dillinger understands—pertinent to this time of the Depression—that the public has no love for institutions like banks, and his robberies are thus heralded by the folk culture. He does, however, show interest in a possible train robbery that Karpis is casing. "It's a big score," Karpis says, "the kind of thing you go away on."

This addresses a peculiar facet about Karpis (which made him interesting to Mann to begin with; Mann wrote a screenplay about Karpis in the late 1970s): the end of his criminality is escape into leisure, representative of the general working man. He doesn't necessarily like what he's doing, but it's the only thing that he *can* do in order to catch up with time lost in prison. Kidnappings offer bigger payoffs than bank robberies, where the risk outweighs the reward. Karpis was considered the most intelligent of the public enemies, his strategy mapped out like a life plan. He wanted to create a new identity, financed by his heists, and then live quietly and comfortably. This is the same objective as Frank in *Thief*, McCauley in *Heat*, and suggested by Crockett to Isabella in *Miami Vice*. It's good to cash out before it's too late. "You can't outrun gravity," Crockett says. Time is luck and luck runs out.

Asked by Karpis about the future, Dillinger admits he doesn't have one. Mann brings particular attention to how Depp says it by raising the volume on the line: "No plans." Dillinger, much like this film's structure, is so focused on the present moment as opposed to the past or future that "there ain't no thinking about tomorrow." This man has the ability to execute perfect robberies and has expertly molded his legacy among the public, but he is so caught in the sensational celerity of life, outrunning time while making up for the time he's lost, that he has no ability to brake and plan for the coming week. Dillinger is still a ne'er-do-well, but with money now, he evades stasis whether in prison or the outside.

It's here where Dillinger first sees Billie Frechette dancing in a red dress. He approaches her, putting on a charming smile and uttering movie dialogue: "I don't know why you gave that fella the go-by," he says referring to her previous dancing partner, "but I'm glad you did." Is this clumsy hackneyed screenwriting, inserting a token love story within the gangster mural? Much of Dillinger and Frechette's dialogue will *feel scripted*, and we will even see it scripted, as federal agents look at transcriptions of their phone conversations. But the romance between Dillinger and Frechette was very real, according to both eyewitnesses and those transcripts, and the nature of the relationship calls attention to a subtext in *Public Enemies* relating to amatory cinema. In a film where dialogue is often muted (there's very little of it in the first fifteen minutes), Dillinger's direct address to Frechette indicates that his words in fact have something to do with a romantic image of himself that he has constructed with the help of his love for the movies, related to a role in which he is casting himself as a protector of his leading lady. The actuality of his identity matters less than the performance of this role, so he stumbles over himself when she asks his name. "Jack," he says clumsily, beginning to dance with her as the house singer (Diana Krall) sings "Bye, Bye Blackbird."

Later on, he will make her repeat romantic "line readings" to him on the phone (the same moment we see scripted onto paper), echoing something forced out of Purvis by Hoover, and so linking these two relationships as casting for important roles (Hoover and Purvis's movie taking place on public spaces of newspapers, Dillinger and Frechette's as something ethereal and private, official spaces against subjective ones). What's interesting to observe is Dillinger talking to Billie about herself, but only through *his* eyes, praising her beauty in such a way that he seems to be creating her right there on the dance floor, wasting no time in casting her with a hurried impatience similar to Frank in *Thief* (who tells Jessie, "Let's cut all the mini-moves and the bullshit and get on with this big romance!" Similarly, in his DVD commentary for *Heat*, Mann says that Ashley Judd's Charlene was essentially the woman a lonely inmate like her husband, Chris Shihirlis [Val Kilmer], would invent while incarcerated). Dillinger is "catching up," he tells her, and like the movie, he has no time to give expository details about himself. He has no time to dwell on Billie from a distance, and letting the relationship grow organically. He has a definite picture of fulfillment: he sees it, he wants it, it fits into his romantic collage and frame, he takes it—only with as much irresistible charm and performative ability as seen in one of his robberies. Those robberies reinforce the performative nature of the Dillinger gang when Van Meter flirts with one of their hostages (Emilie de Ravin) by telling her, "When I'm not doing this I'm a scout for the movies."

These characters, in love with the mass-cult experience of movies, have sublimated movie romance into their everyday lives, because that higher culture of romance— however unreal—stands in opposition to the alternative reality of the Depression. In the 1930s, the movies were a shelter. They could be liberating. Dillinger calls Billie "dark and beautiful, like that bird in that song." She is a work of art to him, the body electric registered by the camera and adored by the onlooker. This idea finds its conclusion at the Biograph, where Dillinger watches *Manhattan Melodrama*. But what is mythology and what is reality in this cycle of influence? Blackbird and Billie, Clark Gable and Johnny, Myrna Loy and Billie? Mann is not denigrating these mythic forms in our culture of screened images in accordance to how the subject interprets those images. The exchange is a mutual heightening of art and life, romance and being.

This commentary on the medium continues when Dillinger and Frechette exit the Aragon. There's a jump-cup as they approach the sidewalk, a formal maneuver taking us temporarily out of the romance and reminding us that this is a film. It also, in this movie of incessant forward movement, suggests the transcending qualities of this relationship, as for a small moment the characters have broken the deterministic flux, subverting the cinematic and temporal laws of gravity. The image of Dillinger and Billie breaks from the previous instant, indicating a new beginning for these two. If the Goldenthal score swelling at two points during the romance feels disarmingly melodramatic, it is because the music is a projection of Dillinger's cinematic sense, in love with the melodrama of movies. At a syndicate restaurant, the camera lingers on Billie in close-up as she looks at Dillinger (much like the Myrna Loy close-ups we see later in *Manhattan Melodrama*). As they optically savor each other, they're separated from the rest of the space, dwelling within a constructed fantasy. They're even removed from us. Later at a Miami racetrack, Dillinger folds their romance into a final scenario. "I ain't going anywhere, and neither are you. I'm going to die an old man in your arms." The music swells as they kiss, the world left far behind as horses cross the finish line and every other character in the frame rises to see the winner. Mann's treatment of the romance is a commentary on our cinematic experiences of love and companionship, which we use to form apperceptions and reactions to our own relationships in the real world. Is Billie simply an agent for Dillinger's desire? Yes, she is. This is a film about subjectivity, and Dillinger has invented Billie Frechette, just as the folk culture/FBI has invented "John Dillinger." Mann plays with this idea by having Dillinger identify with the female voice on the radio (Billie's namesake, Holiday) when thinking about his love, and later the symbolism is more transparent, when Billie's freedom from FBI surveillance is accomplished by assuming the guise of a man, absconding with Dillinger as federal agents are duped. She *is* Dillinger and he *is* Billie.[1]

The syndicate restaurant has the same vertical columns as the prison that opened the film, as if the brutal arena has been dressed up. There, Dillinger gives his identity away to Billie: "I'm John Dillinger, I rob banks." Wanting to implant himself in a "real" relationship with her means that he must

---

1. People create their reality as filmmakers do, life reinforcing art reinforcing life, each perception between human optics and photographic manipulation an expanding, elegant universe unto itself. The HD video presentation of a '30s gangster saga addresses its method of presenting an oft-filmed subject while also remaining the work of a tireless director. Mann's decision to relay formal ideas musically is a common feature in his films, however overlooked. As an interesting point of comparison, the melodramatic music used to separate the lovers from the simulacrum of *Public Enemies* is not unlike the synthesized Tangerine Dream score highlighting Frank's triumph after his climactic heist in *Thief*, where Mann films Frank, Jessie, and Frank's partner Barry (Jim Belushi) as if they were in a commercial, luxuriating on a California beach. It implies the dimension of fantasy. At the end of this triumphant, synth-heavy sequence, we see the nondiegetic music is in fact coming from Frank's expensive home stereo. It is artificial and manufactured. The score is inverted by the hard guitar rock used during the film's finale, where the nihilism of Frank's revolt rejects the hyperreal dictates of his capitalist exploiters: between nothingness and being real in a place where reality is dictated by a corrupt system, and he chooses nothingness. This Brechtian use of music score is employed by Mann elsewhere, such as the gentle scene between Max and Ann in *Collateral*, where Groove Armada's "Hands of Time" fools us into thinking that it is coming from Max's taxi radio, when in fact it is the song scoring Max's psychological experience of warmth with Anna. Whatever music is being played on the radio is unheard by *Collateral*'s audience; it's identified by both characters as being classical. Elsewhere, incongruent cuts in *Manhunter*'s climax reflects psychopath Francis Dollarhyde's unwinding, the film itself "having a nervous breakdown," as Aradillas and Seitz point out in their video essay, "Zen Pulp, Pt. Four." *Blackhat* similarly has blips and jumps, itself a digital film constructed of code telling the story where code is "erratic" and "overwritten." Our subjectivity triumphs objectivity, for better or worse.

relate to her in good faith, again like Frank in *Thief*, who can't begin his romance until he has—emphatically—come clean with Jessie. This contrasts to doomed relationships in Mann's work, like with serial killer Francis Dollarhyde (Tom Noonan) and blind photo-lab coworker Reba (Joan Allen) in *Manhunter*, who engages in an affair with him oblivious to his pathological secret life as a butcher of families; in *Heat*, between McCauley and budding graphic designer Eady (Amy Brennenman), who falls in love with a man she takes to be a businessman working in metals; the marriage between Jeffrey and Liane Wigand (Russell Crowe, Diane Venora) falls apart in *The Insider* because he is unable to tell her essential information, such as his firing from a tobacco firm, and then his ruinous agreement to break a confidentiality agreement for a CBS interview; between Max and Annie in *Collateral*, where his plan to design a limousine business attracts her, but the fact that he will probably never go through with it impedes him from daring to call her; and Crockett and Isabella in *Miami Vice*, a relationship founded on mutual duplicity that "has no future." Ironically in *Thief*, though Frank is honest with Jessie, they are also doomed because their relationship is grounded on a financial relationship of dishonest exchanges with crime boss Leo (Robert Prosky), who provides Frank with wealth, home, and child but at the cost of dehumanizing exploitation. Mann's individuals struggle for transparency while in a default of duplicity. Tellingly, lovemaking in his films often shares the commonality of the lovers usually still wearing clothes—Frank and Jessie in *Thief*; Will and Molly (Kim Greist), and Francis and Reba in *Manhunter*; Vincent and Justine in *Heat*; Ali and Sonji (Jada Pinckett-Smith) in *Ali*; Crockett and Isabella in *Miami Vice*; Nicholas Hathaway (Chris Hemsworth) and Chen Lien (Tang Wei) in *Blackhat*; and John Dillinger and Billie Frechette in *Public*

Enemies, where the lovemaking is almost held in abstract rapture, constructed with jump-cuts and total breaks in continuity, choreographed expressively with the composition selections, interrupted by Billie's voice-over explaining her past. What happens here, and often in Mann, is the body in motion ascending to erotic transcendence, independent from carnal pleasure.[2] Their physicality together relates to issues of time, how the romance over-steps temporality's imprisoning boundaries, tangible material physics aspiring to exist outside of abrading time. But however exhilarating the rush of connection, Mann's lucidity juxtaposes that peak sensation against gravity that reminds the audience these lovers never can fully know the extended object of desire and, whether worn out by duplicity or the struggle for transparency, they really live as they will die—alone.

Billie's backstory is given through fragmented voice-over (much like Mann will next do in 2015's *Blackhat*, withholding even more information). She grew up on an Indian reservation, moving from church to church. She acted in plays, so her performative abilities extend from literal stages to good time flop houses and, more broadly, as an oppressed Native American assuming the mores and appearances of the colonizing white culture that abused her. We can't know how interested he is, considering his faith in whatever is "right now." Earlier when Billie says she doesn't know Dillinger, he quickly responds, "I was raised on a farm in Indiana; my momma died when I was three; my daddy beat the hell out of me because he had no idea how to raise me; I love movies, baseball, good clothes, fast cars,

---

2. Seitz's series of video essays on Mann, "Zen Pulp," is an invaluable commentary on the director, particularly an installment focusing on the relationships Mann's male protagonists have with women. "When the action shifts to the bedroom, [Mann] becomes a religious filmmaker," Seitz points out. (Seitz, "Zen Pulp, Pt. 3").

whiskey, and you. What else you need to know?" His selection and certainty of Billie as leading lady has her mention, "Boy, you're in a hurry," which applies to the film itself. For Dillinger, a day is a long time, as indicated by his hotel migrations. From fragments, in character and in the construction of scenes (taking cue from Robert Bresson), there's a stubbornness to Mann's approach that trusts an audience to intuit and complete the larger picture, or challenges them for their need of absolute knowledge and how they're accustomed to translate "character" and "plot" development in a feature film.

"It's not where you're from," Dillinger says to Billie. "It's where you're going." The irony is Dillinger isn't necessarily "going" anywhere except toward more movement in the present. His desired destination where past, present, and future intersect in a state of pure fulfillment, is in lovemaking with Billie and savoring her image. The Billie Holiday lyrics for "Love Me or Leave Me" is a chorus commentary, "I want your love but I don't want to borrow / Have it today to give back tomorrow," expressing the longing for something immutable that is not controlled by time. "Where are you going?" she asks. "Anywhere I want," he answers. He's telling the truth, to an extent, but he must always be "going." He will never stay comfortably "anywhere," and that "anywhere" is a utopian abstraction, a place he names as "off the map" later, a fantasy closed off to the governing, looming shadow of Hoover's modernist system. Freedom here is not necessarily economic freedom as in "free enterprise," but *freedom from* cruel economics, just as it is *freedom from* the burden of politics.

6

HOOVER'S CINEMA OF CONTROL

Following his capture in Arizona, Dillinger is flown to Chicago in an immense Ford TriMotor aircraft, Mann inserting seemingly archival black-and-white footage (it isn't). Mann's HD cameras pay particular attention to the now-ancient cameras shooting the action and archiving reality onto public celluloid, preserving the moment in a newsreel that resurrects the subject's (Dillinger's) mystique upon projection. In Indiana, Dillinger is empowered by the camera and microphones (much like Muhammad Ali). John Dillinger is in complete control as an actor in his own self-scripted movie, as Sheriff Holly (Lili Taylor) and the District Attorney Robert Estill (Alan Wilder) are humorously diminished, the latter even putting his arm around Dillinger. For the first time in front of microphones and movie cameras, Dillinger performs with his wit and charm, telling his story with deliberate pathos, masterfully manipulating the public through the lens. At his trial, defended by Louis Piquett (Peter Gerety), and with dialogue mostly taken verbatim from history, Dillinger is painted as an enslaved victim of injustice, his shackles carrying reference to "the tyranny of the czars." Piquett cleverly fools Sheriff Holly into making the court believe Dillinger will be securely contained within her Crown Point jail, and that there is no need for him to be sent to the state penitentiary, where escape is impossible and the electric chair waits.

What follows is a fascinating sequence of movement toward escape as Dillinger, helped by a hulking inmate named Herbert Youngblood (Michael Bentt), goes through eight locked doors. The obstacles are visually presented from the outside in, the scene beginning with an establishing shot of the jail, which looks more like a fort. Inside, Dillinger waits for a janitor to come through the holding cell. He bolts and holds the janitor down while shoving a gun into his neck—the pistol later revealed to be nothing more than sculpted washboard. The raw technique mixes with the performance of a natural born actor who convinces his unwilling fellow players that he will kill them unless they follow his demands. He keeps their backs to him, making the gun invisible but present. Youngblood covers him, holding down multiple guards at once. Performance is everything in *Public Enemies*.

The first door open, Youngblood subdues the harmless janitor and Dillinger grabs the next guard, quick enough so that the gun is not seen and that the two bodies—Dillinger and the officer—are already against the second door. The process repeats from door to door, with Dillinger finally getting to an armory. "I knew it wasn't real," a guard says as Dillinger puts on a hat and heads into the garage, exiting through the last barrier in a car "with the new V-8." Passing through all of these impediments with two hostages and Youngblood, the most suspenseful adversary in the sequence is probably a traffic light. The Ford remains inconspicuous to the array of armed men on the sidewalk, a police car similarly halted at the light. The green blips up and, passing the cop car, Dillinger puts the V-8 into gear.

The fugitive sings "The Last Roundup" to his hostages: "Get along lil'doggies, get along, get along," a cheerful tune that we see forever related with his character once the hostages are freed and share their stories with the media. Hoover listens in disgust, the image accentuating his peculiar relationship with Tolson during a back-and-forth rack-focus between them. Through a post-human, telepathic means these two are communicating and, to an extent, running the country.

Hoover and the syndicate have reacted. The safe houses are closed off. Chief Zarkovich tells Dillinger, "I'm only taking orders" as he waves him away. Sanctuary nests that were essential are not off limits because the system—whether government (the Bureau is recording Billie Frechette's phone calls with men outside her apartment) or the syndicate (they will not protect the public enemies any longer)—has interests that are more important than the humane exchanges we saw earlier. Dillinger confronts Nitti's front man, Deandre, about these new syndicate rules. He's taken to a primitive call center, a set mirroring the Bureau's spooky surveillance room, where the passing information brings in as much money every day, day after day, as one highline Dillinger bank robbery. This is a new bookmaking monopoly. "These phones equal money," Deandre explains, as the system, determining the nature of dialogue and relationships, is tied to its exploding techno-capital infrastructure. Because Nitti pays the cops to stay out of this call center, it can continue to run without delay. The only obstruction to this flowing capital is Dillinger or other "outsider" gangsters who are not part of the criminal syndicate. Nitti has forbidden safe havens, medical help, and financial assistance, and would probably wish them dead because of the extra heat they attract (a historical example being Verne Miller, who was partially responsible for the Kansas City Massacre). "We ain't harboring you no more," Deandre says sternly, but as we see with Purvis, he's a man of two minds. He whispers to Dillinger, "But do you need anything to tide you over?" With Deandre, as with many people existing in bad faith, Dillinger is talking to two separate people in one body.

Hoover's Bureau is increasingly amoral as it reaches for a kind of Hobbesian, sovereign super control. With dripping venom, Hoover confronts Purvis. "Hamilton has a 36-year-old sister, arrest her." He then lists other family members related to Dillinger's gang and how they all must be apprehended, regardless of whether or not they have been in contact with the fugitives. "Hamilton hasn't seen his sister in years," Purvis says. "*Then create informants,*" Hoover snaps back. Hoover understands that the apparatus is the new liquidator and creator of reality. "We are in a modern age," he whispers. "As they say in Italy nowadays, *take off the white gloves!*" Making reference to Mussolini's Italy, Hoover walks away from Purvis and assumes a totally different countenance, stepping to his marker in front of cameras with a dozen uniformly dressed "young crime fighters," presenting them all with badges for their work.

The image changes into celluloid screened in an auditorium, viewed by Dillinger, Hamilton, and Van Meter, who are now joined by Tommy Carroll and Ed Shouse. The children that Hoover awards are emblematic of a homogenous America of subservience with perspectives conditioned by the state—the public perspective, as opposed to individual conscientiousness. The poetry of John Dillinger as folk hero meets the subterfuge of Hoover's mechanical conditioning, initiating people as automatons in a fascistic culture. We notice that Hoover's presence in the cinema is the prelude to a Bureau-sponsored newsreel detailing the public enemies, including Dillinger.[1]

"They may be in this theater," the booming narrator tells the audience. Mann cuts, wryly, to Dillinger and company looking on. "They may be sitting amongst you," and the auditorium lights go on. Dillinger is still, only his eyes scanning. "Turn to your left," the voice directs. Everyone in the audience, with the exception of Dillinger, turns to the left. "Turn to your right." Everyone turns right.

The apparatus of control has its strongest weaponry in the cinema, something reflecting back onto us as viewers of *Public Enemies*. How do we interact here in front of this flickering behemoth? To quote Herbert Marcuse, "Technological rationality reveals its political character as it becomes the great vehicle of better domination, creating a truly totalitarian universe in which society and nature, mind and body are kept in a state of permanent mobilization for the defense of this universe."[2] The people in this movie theater are not engaged with what's on the screen. They're lulled into a trance. This is textually significant and will find its counterpart toward the end as John Dillinger watches *Manhattan Melodrama*, a clunky mass-market Hollywood product. What differentiates the newsreels from the

---

1. From the traffic light to the movie theater, "A technological rationale is the rationale of domination itself," this from Adorno and Horkheimer, "Culture Industry," 1. "Life in the late capitalist era is a constant initiation rite. Everyone must show that he wholly identifies himself with the power which is belaboring him. . . . The miracle of integration, the permanent act of grace by the authority who receives the defenseless person—once he has swallowed his rebelliousness—signifies fascism" (ibid., 17–18).

2. Marcuse, *One-Dimensional Man*, 20.

melodrama? What differentiates the automatic-response viewers in this scene from Dillinger at the Biograph?

Punctuating this first theater scene is a newsreel feature on Ethiopia, a historical reference tying the propaganda we've just seen to Hoover's endorsement of Mussolini's Italy and the tide of futurism, as in 1934 Italy would indeed take off its "white gloves" while warring with Ethiopia in establishing its empire. This ties to the League of Nations mentioned earlier, and subsequently with a Will Rogers radio broadcast where there's opposition to government spending, all reflecting an anxiety about imperial establishment. Surely, FDR's administration needed to establish a federal system in order to deal with interstate criminals, just as the New Deal needed to be implemented to save the economy; but the attitudes and ideas of whatever is constructing this pervasive, gigantic structure, determining its moral character, the mind in the machine, is more important (FDR? Or Hoover and Mussolini?)

The way of the future has overlaid Dillinger's dexterity in mastering time and space. He wants to break Pierpont and Mackley out of prison again; he wants to get back with Billie; and he's desperate for a big score. And being desperate he's forced to join forces with the erratic reprobate Baby Face Nelson, whom Dillinger does not respect. Nelson has cased a Sioux Falls bank that will pay off $800,000. This, in addition to Karpis's train robbery, will finance Dillinger's dreams of reuniting with his friends and his lover. But desperation does not pay off. Nelson is more focused on shooting people outside the bank than making sure the job is done efficiently; he's another actor who gleefully plays up to the spectacle of his reputation. The gang is unexpectedly flanked from above, and Dillinger is shot in the arm while Carroll is mortally wounded and left behind. Nelson keeps firing and will not get in the car, resulting in more collateral damage, detrimental to Dillinger's reputation. He has to grab Nelson and throw him inside in order for the group to escape. The risk was not worth the reward. Instead of $800,000, they've taken $46,000, or $8,000 a man.

The action here reaches its crescendo. The sound hushes as the gang drives into the forest, trees shining on the car's paint. Goldenthal's music rises and we drift with the vehicle into thick night. They come to Little Bohemia in Northern Wisconsin, and one of the most infamous battles in the history of American law enforcement. After splitting the money, Dillinger shares a quiet moment with Hamilton. "We need to leave tomorrow morning," he says. Hamilton says something bizarre. "You'll be all right," which means that Hamilton has an inclination of his demise. "When your time's up, your time's up," he tells Dillinger. "And my time's up." The narrative has sustained itself on criminals running from existential realities, and Hamilton is the only one who, before being mortally wounded, seems ready to let go and give up. He's a Hegelian wind-up toy, a doomed outlaw replicant from *Blade Runner* exhausted and awaiting expiration. There's an eeriness, an uncanniness, to several moments in *Public Enemies*, and we see it here with Hamilton much as we see it with Hoover, Purvis, and Nitti elsewhere (and Floyd, who says to Purvis, "I believe you have killed me" with a curious affectation).

The same strangeness is exhibited by Purvis in the following scene, as agents torture Carroll, who is in terrible pain from his head wound. Filmed in a close-up as Carroll screams behind him, Purvis is blankly open-mouthed as if his consciousness was being rebooted and processing an alien form of programming. This is a terrifying and remorseless cruelty far removed from the scientific method that he espoused earlier. The ends have come to justify whatever means, and Hoover's insistence that the "white gloves" come off has amounted to a man whose integrity has been displaced by a corporate, technologically dictated identity. He obstructs a doctor from administering drugs that would alleviate Carroll's pain, something explicitly anti-scientific.[3]

Purvis's ineffectual leadership is central to the Little Bohemia raid. Surrounding the resort and ignoring the strategic advice of Winstead, Purvis opens fire on a group of men who've recently left the bar and are preparing to drive off. Out of his element in the dark, Purvis has mistakenly killed two civilians and possibly injured another. Galvanized by the gunfire, Dillinger hops off his bed (again, rest and leisure interrupted), while Mann cuts to a framed portrait above his bed, of a man riding a wild horse, a significant Bressonian detail. The ensuing gunfight reflects real details of the massacre, where it was so dark that individuals on both sides of the law, in addition to civilians, did not know on whom they were firing. Nelson, Shouse, and Van Meter reach one exit, and Dillinger and Hamilton take the other.

Racing into the woods, they're stalked by Winstead who, in contrast to Purvis, is totally coordinated in this environment. Fired upon by Dillinger, Winstead ducks and somersaults on the ground, re-poised and ready with an aimed rifle. As he runs into the trees he would seem to be vulnerable to Dillinger and Hamilton—except he's disappeared. The vaporous mist around them suggests how they're entangled with something ethereal as opposed to clunking and mechanical.[4]

3. Remembering how in *The Insider*, Jeffrey Wigand defines the man of science as someone distinct from the man of business; the man of science would not allow a person to be harmed.

4. In *The Last of the Mohicans*, the Mohicans and their principle enemy, the Huron Magua (Wes Studi), meld and move with the

Just as mysteriously as he disappeared, Winstead materializes and shoots Hamilton. Dillinger helps his friend to safety down a slope. Winstead was right about his recommendation to Purvis regarding reinforcements and properly blockading an area with "a lot of real estate." Nelson, meanwhile, stops a Bureau car driven by Baum who, like Purvis, lacks the foresight to suspect an ambush. Nelson ferociously fires on Baum, pulls him out of the car, and shoots him again. Nelson, like Dillinger, takes his cues from the movies (earlier we see him imitating James Cagney), and he delivers classic movie dialogue here, "I'm going to give it to you high and give it to you low."

Purvis flags down a car and pursues Nelson, who's picked up Shouse and Van Meter. The scene ends with Purvis firing into the night, Nelson's car spinning out into a ditch, the impact killing Shouse instantly (in the passenger seat, the doltish Shouse appeared to be experiencing the escape with the detachment of a passive film viewer). Van Meter and Nelson are both killed by Purvis and the agents, Nelson's death an over-the-top tempest of gunfire commensurate to his megalomaniacal character.[5]

Dillinger has broken into a pharmacy to get Hamilton medication. "Haven't you ever seen a man die?" the

---

natural environment as if they were a part of it, and so very differently from the English and French soldiers, estranged from an appreciation of nature who think of it abstractly, through policy and treaties ("British policy makes the world England"). In a confused skirmish set in the thick of nature, Purvis in *Public Enemies* has killed innocent civilians, just as Duncan in *The Last of the Mohicans* comes close to accidentally killing Chingachgook (Russell Means). Winstead and Dillinger, however, seem to be the only characters who know where they are in this confusing geography.

5. Both Nelson and Van Meter were in fact killed after Dillinger, Nelson dying in a fashion not unlike his death portrayed in the film, Van Meter being brutally slain by police in St. Paul, Minnesota.

lethargic Hamilton asks. "You gotta let go, John. Billie too." This stops Dillinger. Hamilton's death reminds him that his time is running out. His stubborn determination to flee and fight is pointless when he has nowhere left to go and no one left to see. He has also, it seems, run out of space. Congress has just passed a National Crime Bill that will prosecute interstate criminals, sparking Nitti's ire. Federal power is now coast to coast. "Wake up!" Nitti complains to Deandre. "That's what we are!" The corporate body of control now being coast-to-coast, interstate, indicates the conquest of the frontier.

Billie absconds from her apartment by fooling sur-veilling agents with a body double. Disguising herself as a man, Billie walks into Chicago's streets and is reunited with Dillinger, hiding in a parked car. Mann then places these lovers in an abstraction of space. At 4 a.m., before sand and driftwood in front of Lake Michigan's nocturnal black, they talk as if in a dream. Dillinger offers a plan. He will finish Karpis's train robbery and they'll leave. "Where?" she asks, wondering if it's Cuba or South America. Dillinger's answer reflects the empty, black space behind them. They will slide "off the map," as he puts it. This kind of sacred space to which Dillinger refers was the frontier of early America, the demise of which was forecasted by the Chingachgook at the conclusion of *The Last of the Mohicans*.[6] By 1934, there is no frontier left, no space or private sphere where one is "beholden to none," as Hawkeye puts it earlier in that film.

6. There have been three official versions of *The Last of the Mohicans* released, Mann's first (theatrical) and final (blu ray) cuts deleting Chingachgook's final words to Hawkeye and Cora after they've laid to rest Chingachgook's only biological son, Uncas, Mann trusting the image and expressions to convey the melancholy message. A second DVD cut from 2002 literalizes the feeling with his dialogue as he says, "One day there will be no more frontier."

Billie agrees to take this ride with Dillinger, a journey not necessarily suited for reality so much as for the imagination—and the movies. This space "off the map" is analogous to the abstract future always arriving as the present, the future remaining fixed out of grasp. Tangible "meat-space," as William Gibson defines it (and so anticipating where Mann will go with *Blackhat*), has been eaten up by modernity and there is nowhere to move. The celeritous rate of change is midwifing an interminable Right Now of "zero history," to use another Gibson phrase.

Using telephone surveillance, the Bureau apprehends Billie more easily than Dillinger was able to free her. Going to meet a Dillinger contact at a liquor store, she is cornered by the portly Agent Reinecke (Adam Mucci). "How'd you get here?" he demands. "A taxi," she nervously answers. Dillinger watches from outside. The agents and police are oblivious to his presence. Billie is driven away.

The scene shows that John Dillinger, as a flesh and blood meat-space entity, is not real. His reality is not in his body but tied to his *public* image in official photographs, mugshots, newspaper clippings, newsreels, etc. Among the public he belongs to the air, to the media, screen, and ether. He is a ghost, a virtual character shuffling between spaces in this new Right Hegelian system where being a citizen counts more than subjectivity.

In a later scene, Dillinger accompanies a new girlfriend, Polly Hamilton (Leelee Sobieski), to city hall so that she can get her waitress license. He chooses to enter the police department with her, even entering the police's Dillinger Squad room. He has his gun in his pants and doesn't hesitate to explore the officers' desks. On the soundtrack is the wordless wail of Blind Willie Johnson and his "Dark Was the Night, Cold Was the Ground," influenced by Christ preparing for his death at Gethsemane.[7] Dillinger is confronting his myth, and the *myth* is his *reality*. As the camera scans over photographs of Dillinger, note how we haven't seen a personal photo of him throughout the entire movie. Recalling the horse track scene in Miami, where Deandre invites Dillinger to come to a special syndicate club, Dillinger even says, "No pictures," meaning that he didn't want his picture taken. On one level this indicates that he doesn't want his image associated with amoral syndicate criminals, but it also suggests that, in the context of this film, he is separate from the personalized, unique, unreplicated image, that which has aura. He belongs to something larger, either as criminal in the system, or as hero in myth, denoting the "off the map" place that America cherishes and sings as its own Whitmanian song of self, muffled though persevering in modernity's blizzard of feedback.

"What's the score?" Dillinger asks the circle of cops on this hot July day, surrounding a radio. "Cubs 3–2, seventh inning," one answers. Dillinger smiles. He is a transmigrating spirit with no past or future whose history is not contained in biological relationships but on office paper and system photos. He is the institution's bastard child and usurper. This idea again corresponds to the filmmaker's method of framing Dillinger's story not as conventional film biography, but as a consideration of the medium through which we are experiencing him. Mann wants us to think about the character's mythology, and how we experience cinema, in a new way.[8]

7. Cinephiles may recognize the song from Pier Paolo Pasolini's *The Gospel According to St. Matthew* (1964), perhaps the most well-regarded film dealing with the life of Jesus Christ.

8. While giving props to Mann for how strange his approach is, for expensive film biographies it's not unprecedented. Probably the most formidable and challenging approach to a film biography, also

Dillinger's ghostly unreal-ness hovers over Reinecke's abusive interrogation of Billie, whom he slaps repeatedly while she's tied up in the Chicago Bureau office. His unwillingness to allow Billie to use the restroom indicates how the Bureau and its unethical practices are insensitive to basic human freedom (and is there anything more basic to freedom than being able to go when you have to go?). Billie gives up, fessing to Reinecke that Dillinger is staying at an apartment on Addison Street. The agents go there to discover blank walls and no furniture. An incensed Reinecke returns and takes a phone book to Billie's head, a curt metaphor of a mass of government sanctioned identities and spaces in opposition to the privacy "off the map" desired by John Dillinger and Billie Frechette.

Purvis's secretary Doris Rogers (Rebecca Spence), who has been greatly disturbed by Billie's treatment, serves as a reminder to Purvis of his chivalric upbringing: "Mr. Purvis, those men cannot treat a woman like that." Purvis, who's become increasingly numb over the past two hours, nods at her inference and, with Winstead's help, stops Reinecke.

---

on a digital canvas (in two formally contrastive parts, as if the whole was engaged in its own dialectic), is Steven Soderbergh's *Che* (2008). Over the course of four hours, Soderbergh withholds most background information on his character (excellently played by Benicio Del Toro) regarding the makeup of his beliefs or private thoughts, laying out the most disciplined and fascinating of epic procedurals. Just a dozen minutes before the film's conclusion, as Che is in prison and awaiting execution, we at last get some personal disclosure as he talks to the man guarding him. He then asks his guard, "Will you untie me?" Soderbergh's Che, like Mann's Dillinger, has to be forever in movement, his reality tied in with a myth related to his enigmatic inability to be tied down and clearly defined by an audience that craves definition—audiences were warmer to 2006's more cuddly and facile Guevara biography, Walter Salles's *The Motorcycle Diaries*. Also like with *Public Enemies*, Soderbergh gives particular attention to the evolving technology used by Che's enemies to finally catch him.

Untying Billie, he tells her the bathroom's down the hall. "I can't walk," she limply cries. In a deeply moving gesture, he lifts her up and carries her to the restroom. The scene is incredibly touching not because of Billie's pitiful state so much as Purvis's. It's the last noble gasp afforded a virtuous man betraying his morality. His compliance with his employer has victimized this woman and other innocents.

Then begins the film's denouement. Purvis acts in conjunction with the syndicate and Chicago police as Zarkovich makes a deal with Nitti. Ana Sage is going to be deported to Romania; she is willing to help Purvis (and so the syndicate) capture and kill Dillinger if it means she will be able to stay in America. "I want guarantee," she repeats in a private meeting with Purvis. It's a guarantee he is unwilling—or unable—to give her (he cannot flatly lie). Purvis says that he will do the best he can for her but he *will* guarantee that if she does not cooperate (and Purvis emphasizes his seriousness by not using contractions) he will make sure that she is out of the country within forty-eight hours. She agrees and the trap is set. Aligning herself with power structures, Ana Sage will commit her own contractual sin in this betrayal of Dillinger's trust.[9]

9. The idea of asking large corporations for contractual guarantees is another Mannian motif corresponding to Frankfurt School ideas, always concluding with the system not making good on its language: Leo in *Thief* ("There is no discussion"); the FBI to Will Graham in *Manhunter*; the imperialist generals to Native Americans and colonial frontiersmen in *The Last of the Mohicans*; the corporate criminal Van Zandt (William Fichtner) in *Heat*; the Brown and Williamson tobacco company and CBS to Jeffrey Wigand and Lowell Bergman in *The Insider*; the FBI and the Nation of Islam to Muhammad Ali in *Ali*; Vincent to Max in *Collateral*; the FBI and the panoptical Columbian drug lord to the undercover individuals in *Miami Vice*; the U.S. Department of Justice and the Chinese government to Hathaway's team in *Blackhat*. True to form—and while the outcome isn't relayed in

the film—after cooperating with the FBI, Ana Sage was nevertheless deported. Trust, already negated by the rules of film noir, is ridiculed with extreme prejudice by the types of post-human organizations Mann highlights.

7

DILLINGER'S CINEMA OF LIBERATION

Accenting the religious overtones of Dillinger's last day, "Dark Was the Night, Cold Was the Ground" once again adorns the soundtrack as Dillinger shaves and readies himself, his grooming a ritual concluding with a glance at his time-piece, where across from the clock is an image of Billie, the only personal photograph we see in the film. This sentimental trinket defies the Modern's sway of Zero History, a prayer of love's fulfillment whispering through Dillinger's nadir, expressed in the film's other Billie Holliday song, "The Man I Love," where the man in question is always in the future, "someday," in dreams. The only place where John Dillinger can experience this fulfillment is the place where we are, also staring at an illusory projection, searching for something authentic, eternal, personal, and real in a mass replicated capitalist object—the movies.

The Biograph Theatre scene works on two levels. As a demonstration of the intensification of movie suspense, it's a brilliant conclusion. But as romance, with Dillinger affirming his dream of love, life, and death "off the map"

73

through movies, it's possibly the zenith of Mann's artistry. For Dillinger, the cinema screen is not escapism or empty projection, but a mirror opening the viewer up to the marvelous subjectivity that he has molded and nurtured through his experiences and relationships, a conduit of self-fashioning and refashioning worthy of Renaissance genius, the model for presenting the self in everyday life, not a channel to enslavement but a portal to transcendence. Dillinger at the cinema is an address to his audience. Mann has an interest in how we react to images, setting into motion a dynamic that follows us outside the theater and may affect positive change and give new perspectives.[1]

Returning to the problematic Frankfurt School ideas of film and mass culture, Herbert Marcuse writes that as long as art has become part of the system, it ceases in questioning it, and thus impedes social change. Poetic language must transcend the "real" world of the society, and in order to transcend that world it must stand opposed to it, questioning it, quelling us out of it. "The truly avant-garde works of literature," Marcuse writes, "communicate the break with communication."[2] What Mann is doing with Dillinger in the climax is not avant-garde, and yet it demonstrates how he, as a major Hollywood director, is sedulously walking a wire to build a major movie entertainment that simultane-

1. How the image affects us is central to *The Insider* and *Ali*, of course, and very complicated in *Manhunter*; the film's whole flashy aesthetic seems to be moving through the scoptophilic cerebral cortex of Francis Dollarhyde. While Mann, like Bresson, immerses us through fractal images while paradoxically suggesting our independence from the image, there's a longing to fuse with the representation, just as Dollarhyde "becomes" William Blake's Red Dragon, or "becomes" wanted, accepted, and desired in the home movies of the strangers he will kill and rearrange, so rewriting his own troubled, abused past.

2. Marcuse, *One-Dimensional Man*, 71.

ously interrogates and rejects popular notions of the status quo of film's established paradigm.[3] The staggering climax inside the Biograph beseeches us to aspire to the images conscientiously, reconciling the mass-produced product with our private histories and elevating the picture and our lives with the media. We are the film, Myrna Loy is Billie Frechette, Marion Cotillard is Billie Frechette and Myrna Loy, and Billie Frechette—and so Myrna Loy and Marion Cotillard—corresponds to someone off the map in our own lives, in another world, their memory sustained by the delirium of faith. So too are we John Dillinger and Melvin Purvis, Red Hamilton and Carter Baum, Walter Dietrich and the woman at the farm, Ana Sage and Polly Hamilton. This most suspenseful part of *Public Enemies*, as Purvis and company prepare to ambush Dillinger, is also when both Dillinger and the entire motion picture feel most contented and rested. The ambush is not, like the other arrests, a brusque interruption. It fits into Dillinger's self-scripted destiny. The dialectic between audience and motion picture, between reality and myth, completes itself.

Dillinger is watching *Manhattan Melodrama*, about a gangster's (Clark Gable) relationship to his law-enforcement friend (William Powell) and the woman between them (Myrna Loy). Dillinger here sees his own life, but not as facile biography. It is the affirmation of his subjectivity and soulfulness, untouched by the Bureau or syndicate. The gangster's name, "Blackie," associates with the "blackbird" of the song during Dillinger's first dance with Billie, who is

3. Released a year before *Public Enemies* was Abbas Kiarostami's *Shirin*, constructed of close-ups on (mostly) women in a theater watching a lavish, sentimental Persian romance. We don't see the conventional film they're watching, but in hearing it and watching their own absorbed reactions, we become an essential player with them, the unseen movie's doggerel transfigured into a magnificent, minimalist poem.

the blackbird of the song, as the blackbird is Blackie, who is John Dillinger, who is Billie Frechette, who is the audience. The riddle of optical adoration, where one is savoring and worshipful of another, overleaps the confines of the controlling "gaze" and becomes the riddle and enigma of oneself as a solitary viewer alone with the myths.

Cinema is elevated to a ceremony of transubstantiation where fixed bodies are resurrected through the mercurial alchemy of speed and light, contradicting the consumption we saw earlier during the newsreel. Dillinger's connection to cinema is a meditative and private one, and the dialogue between his worshipful gaze and Myrna Loy communicates much more than any psychoanalytical monologue. These constructions of studio manufacturing are the co-conspirators of our constructions of reality, the constant revisionists of memory, ironically at a magic place called the Biograph. In film noir, the illusion deceives and dooms us, but Mann, however fatalistic, offers a contemplative, even religious, glimmer of hope and faith in our intelligences as viewers.[4]

4. On his DVD commentary, Mann says, "Audiences, what they intake visually, are quite brilliant. They see more than they even know they see, and it gets processed in the amygdala and other parts of their brain, and a value judgment is rendered that *this feels a certain way, this feels right*, or *this is somewhat artificial and I'll just take it with a grain of salt*. But the trust that you get by an audience in the visual intake, when they're feeling that this is real, this is true, this feels like it would feel . . . is really important. I take it very seriously and it creates a reception for your drama, the story that you tell within the context of that kind of envelope, of a feeling that the world that they're watching is authentic." Mann seems to be complimenting his viewers, but his core belief that everything registers with audiences also points to the precarious responsibility of filmmakers and film studios, who can fatten the audience's cognition. Mann's pursuit of the "feeling," which he gets at through precise detail and quotidian observation comparable to Robert Bresson (take for example, John Dillinger's primitive technique of air conditioning, running his wrists under a cold faucet), places his stories on a certain firmament that

"Die the way you live, all of a sudden," Gable says as he prepares for the electric chair. "Don't drag it out." Dillinger watches transfixed, knowing. His available vector to freedom leads to the same undiscovered country Blackie's approaching. Under the shining movie house lights he is again a real body—and so vulnerable to death, no longer a ghost slipping through the binary data, his last stand photographed in 35 mm (to my knowledge, *Public Enemies'* only scene, other than the hand-cranked newsreels, shot on film). He has a premonition and looks behind him, his eyes catching Reinecke following him. Dillinger glares back, his piercing stare silencing his stalker's frenzied aggression. Reaching for his gun, the final skirmish begins. Winstead is the first of three men to shoot, his bullet going through the back of Dillinger's head and out through the cheek. Purvis, on the other hand, hasn't fired his gun. He's held back, lacking the purposeful elegance and determination required (in this case to shove a woman out of his way). Winstead moves forth swiftly, without hesitation, Blackie's credo of "all of a sudden" in tune with his choreography.

Paralyzed on the ground, Dillinger is mouthing something. Winstead kneels and places his ear close to Dillinger's mouth. We hear "buh-buh . . . buh . . ." and then nothing. John Dillinger is dead. "What he say?" Purvis asks. "Couldn't hear him," answers Winstead. Flares light up as the crowd and photographers move in to witness the site of Dillinger's last stand. Purvis is bathed in light and walks alone, his career apparently saved. Ana Sage fearfully cowers. The camera rests for a second on the shaken, oblivious Polly Hamilton, who didn't know her "Jimmy" was John Dillinger. Everyone on the dense canvas diminishes,

---

stamps them in a viewer's memory, preserving the film through his trust in our deduction.

passing away into the last reel. The camera floats above the Biograph where history fulfilled itself.

The final scene is in a women's correctional facility where Billie serves a two-year sentence. There to meet her is, surprisingly, Winstead. "They say you're the man that killed him," she bitterly remarks. "One of 'em," he says. "So why did you come here? To see all the pain you've caused me?" "No." He pauses, his affect flat but honest. "I came here because he asked me to." He explains that after Dillinger fell, he said something. "And what I think he said was, 'Tell Billie for me, bye bye blackbird.'"

This exchange wasn't based on historical incident. We are, like Billie, taking Winstead's word. Cinema's own relationship to historical facts is problematic (Benjamin referred to Abel Gance's declaration of film's restaging of history to be a great "liquidation") and yet now, as we're barraged by shallow images that mean nothing but advertising and verify public taste, Mann's gesture harbors a cathartic, sacred poetry. These words are sacrosanct, hidden away from Purvis and public record to be stored in a historical prison, recorded and analyzed by the system that would trivialize the speaker. Billie's tears, provoked by private matters, are a final revolt on the closing door that locks her within an institution, signifying the paradox that love and subjectivity may not be truth, but they hold us on a vector independent from an apparatus that works to catalog and control one's private interests, manufacturing identities. Smuggled into the apparatus is the secret knowledge, the ethereal and intimate revelation that subverts the system while atoning the relationship one has to the system, the illuminating spark to be preserved underneath an imperious radar. Regarding cinema's troubling legacy, where the mass-produced image usurps and replaces real life—from its infancy with the Lumiéres' train station to present day virtual reality, gaming, and reality TV—the "blackbird" message to Billie seeks to preserve a tangible materiality within the complex, post-human datum just as digital cinema was on the precipice of being ubiquitous.[5]

Public Enemies fulfills its title, romanticizing and elevating subjectivity in the dance between private and public life. It looks at a time in history when technology accelerated and enabled power structures to override local constructs and private individuals to the extent that it swallowed the mystique of the frontier in its great corporate belly. Hoover's Bureau and the criminal syndicate jointly form a net cast over that frontier, a web matrix processing people in its clockwork machinery. Public enemies pursued freedom from economic and political control, devoted to their comrades and private dreams. Unlike other revisionist period films where characters are de-mythologized or consigned to hagiography, the personages of *Public Enemies* are

5. A worthwhile internet group project devoted to an appreciation of Michael Mann's filmography was "Mann's Sparks" (http://cargocollective.com/mannsparks), where instead of constructing standard video essays, a team of cinephiles (Ryland Walker Knight, Eric Marsh, Sean Gillane, Kurt Walker, and Don Swaynos) took Mann films and edited them to songs from dreampop band Beach House's *Depression Cherry* (2015). Mann's Sparks explores the expressive qualities and themes of the films not didactically, but tonally and visually. *Public Enemies*, set to the song "10:37" and edited by Kurt Walker, stresses the history of the medium in accordance with Mann's HD approach, paralleling the Union Station train arrival with the Lumiéres' *L'Arrivée d'un train en gare de La Ciotat* (1895), which reportedly sent cinematograph viewers fleeing from the screen in fear from the oncoming two dimensional train. Walker's piece points out the significance of images in relation to each other and to the audience, using footage from *Manhattan Melodrama*, where Myrna Loy seems to look directly at the viewer, the back-and-forths between Dillinger, the Biograph movie screen, and Billie in prison alerting the discerning viewer to the obscure fragrance of intimacy underlying publicly exhibited images we take for granted.

visceral, tangible *real* beings aware of their public personae on display and in flux. Its two headlining performances are about performing, one historical performer succeeding before the apparatus with exquisite grace under pressure, the other smothered, a post-script of Purvis's 1961 suicide juxtaposing Dillinger's bang with the mechanical law-man's whimper, Purvis tragically catalogued in time while Dillinger becomes an ageless myth. Returning once again to Walter Benjamin, these characters—and actors—are "not in front of an audience but in front of an apparatus." The split between Dillinger's ascendency and Purvis's decline relates to how the performer "preserves one's humanity in the face of the apparatus," that same apparatus we submit to every day, later applauding the actor, who "[places the apparatus] in the service of his triumph."[6]

There remains a great deal of ambivalence throughout *Public Enemies* and its conclusion, and how it considers the viewer and itself as the output of industrialized production, a construct of modern tools. Michael Mann is a director of contradictions: aesthetic and didactic, abstract and concrete, phantasmagorical and brutally tactile, expressionistic and anthropological, heralding the individual and demanding social responsibility, bold experimenter and studio genre administrator, romantic and futurist, Dillinger freedom seeker and Hoover control freak, outsider and insider. Are we immersed by his digital approach, or are we distracted by it? Maybe he embraces these paradoxes and exhorts us to do likewise, readjusting our eyes to life's expressive capaciousness without and within us. Mann beseeches us to go to the movies as John Dillinger does, unmasking strangers to locate our private mysteries and longings, our eyes wandering through a labyrinthine tool-house where art and life's entanglements cast fugitive

6. Benjamin, *Work of Art*, 30–31.

beams illuminating a way to reconcile ourselves with the beguiling images surrounding and possessing us.

8

BODIES ELECTRIC IN AN ELEGANT
UNIVERSE: BLACKHAT

*P*ublic Enemies was a motion picture showing the future—or our "present"—being fashioned, its period countenance preventing much discussion about its implicit cybernetics. That Michael Mann's follow-up should be an explicit "cyber thriller" (for months on the film production website IMDb, it was listed as "Untitled Michael Mann Cyber Thriller") was considered surprising. Yet while much of the preceding text of this book was researched and written before the release of what would eventually be titled *Blackhat*, it was—both in the abstract and in its unorthodox execution—the motion picture to which Mann had been building toward, I think, perhaps for decades. As such, it has a twofold function in this text.

First, *Blackhat* is an epilogue that closes the circle between *Public Enemies*—a picture released when 35 mm projection was still a norm—and digital cinema's current reign, its formal interest alongside the dramatization of J.

Edgar Hoover's austere law enforcement matrix evolving, over the course of the century, into the infinitely complex specter of cyberspace through which we navigate hourly, and yet to which we biologically and psychologically perhaps haven't adequately adapted. Second, I hope to open a critical discussion about this neglected and strange picture, which stands as an increasingly rare specimen of director-driven material in a production system seemingly geared toward eradicating such curiosities, the frequency of which has accelerated in depletion since *Public Enemies'* release.[1]

On seeing Kubrick's *Dr. Strangelove* in 1964, Mann saw it was possible—however unlikely—that one could be a movie director and not be shackled to anonymous assignments. With his developing luck and talent, Mann became one of the few directors to thrive in the studio system without compromising, the cultural phenomenon of *Miami Vice*

---

1. Relegated—long before the film had completed editing—to the dreaded release slate of mid-January, *Blackhat* failed to open in America's top ten domestic box office. Mann was only one of sundry respected directors who had faltered with audiences in recent years. Other noteworthy examples include Warren Beatty (*Rules Don't Apply*), Steven Spielberg (*The BFG*), and Martin Scorsese (*Silence*), the latter's decision to have his forthcoming film, a $150 million crime drama titled *The Irishman*, financed by the streaming service Netflix, an indicator of massive paradigm change. Meanwhile, the streaming platform of Amazon Studios has become an unexpected sanctuary for a loaded deck of diverse luminaries: Spike Lee (*Chi-Raq*), Woody Allen (*Café Society*), Nicholas Winding Refn (*The Neon Demon*), Whit Stillman (*Love and Friendship*), Kenneth Lonergan (*Manchester by the Sea*), Jim Jarmusch (*Paterson*), Asghar Farhadi (*The Salesman*), Park Chan-Wook (*The Handmaiden*), James Gray (*The Lost City of Z*), and even Terry Gilliam (*The Man Who Killed Don Quixote*). While this trend demonstrates cinema is far from dead, it also augers the end of such films making much of a mark in the communal experience of theatrical moviegoing, granted with a handful of outliers holding the line, e.g. Clint Eastwood (*American Sniper, Sully*), Christopher Nolan (*Dunkirk, Interstellar*).

in the 1980s even making him something of a pop aesthetic conglomerate. Synonymous to his dramatic characters, he maintained freedom while dexterously weaving through studio politics and forces controlling the means of production. *Public Enemies* poetically affirms the mystique of the movie house in a way that cannot help but refract off the director, an irony considering how *Manhattan Melodrama* is antipodal to the type of studio product Mann would strive to create. In *Blackhat*, the movie house is "everywhere," there being no escape from discerning cameras and surveillance, though again, the poetry has to be carefully discerned through the viewer's active participation with the image.

There's a memorable scene in *Heat* where Neil McCauley purchases a score from a mysterious character named Kelso (Tom Noonan), who has a satellite looming over his isolated residence. Kelso is confined to a wheelchair, but, as he explains to Neil, he "knows how to grab" pertinent information flowing throughout the air, such as a bank vault holding $12.2 million in cash. Kelso, whose body is broken and limited to a couple minutes on-screen, is one of the film's major catalysts. He's an antecedent to *Blackhat*'s hackers, a cybertician affecting real-world incident by treading through the ether. He's also an odd double for the director, proposing we adjust our eyes and look more carefully, honing our skills to "grab." Sometimes this is an imperious gaze used to control, but what we have in John Dillinger and in *Blackhat*'s Nicholas Hathaway (Chris Hemsworth), is the strive for an inward truth within the image, optical wings soaring and transcending the "way of the future's" controlling labyrinth.

*

In the Wachowskis' *Matrix* trilogy (1999, 2003, 2004), a hacker discovers the world as he knows it is a computer generated illusion while reality is a dystopia governed by artificial intelligence, feeding off the sleeping human bodies, docile slaves wired into the simulation of 1999, where the AI wears the countenance of J. Edgar Hoover's polished agentry. The encoded world is overpowering, the product of antagonist machinery that an army of freedom-fighting hackers have infiltrated and mastered. The film itself is an exciting fashion show where bullet-speed cameras wow viewers with images that pose and flex with the actors. The form, like the story, is resolutely science fiction, espousing post-structuralist cyborg philosophy, absorbing viewers in its video game-influenced action. There are lines drawn between what's cyberspace and meat-space, the alien dystopic world and the banal 1999 illusion, with the computer programmer combating his tools and reauthoring existence as a new messiah. So when the films have ended, the idea of "cyber" is conveniently tucked away as a plot gambit and fetish fashion line. There remains a binary between human and machine, and the viewer is safe. Ten years later, as if to proclaim cyber-cinema's zenith, David Fincher's *The Social Network* has Napster guru Sean Parker (Justin Timberlake) announce that humankind, previously inhabiting villages, towns, and cities, will soon be making the Internet their home.

But *Blackhat* is distinct in the cyber genre as it is not only *about* technology and cyberspace. It *is* the machine, and through its images, physical geographic space is no longer separate from the "consensual mass hallucination" of cyberspace, as William Gibson defined it in his 1985 novel *Neuromancer*. Hoover's embryo has become a complex and intelligent specimen. In *Blackhat*, we don't live in the Internet so much as the Internet lives here, permeating everything. There's not an otherness to it. It's entrenched in the day-to-day processes of human activity, which is subsumed by post-human or transhuman systems. This includes the cinema, showcasing edges, surfaces, landscapes, screens within screens, bodies in motion being "lean and graceful," much as code is described in the film. Like *The Matrix*, our sense of control is an illusion, but so is cyber/meat-space dualism; the metaphor is, in Mann's hands, tactile. "Cyberspace, it's everting," a character says in Gibson's 2007 novel *Spook Country*, to which another character says in response, mishearing, "Everything?" The cyber condition is a string-theory symphony smearing everything in its interconnectivity and causality, chaos though drawn and written, inscrutable but communicating. We're "dead meat," to use one of the film's many idioms. A pulpy genre film acting as vehicle for the apocalyptic sense of an invasive world hidden among its colonial captors, *Blackhat* is almost a modern reworking of John Carpenter's sci-fi paranoia thriller *They Live* (1988), where special sunglasses enable humans the perspective to see the systems controlling them, bulky Chris Hemsworth in the latter film even evoking pro-wrestler Roddy Piper's presence as Carpenter's hero. This is a new flesh: frightening, strange, and wonderful. *Blackhat* has a disconcerting and dissonant rhythm and flow, a new hum, the stuff of one of the most wildly unconventional genre films released by a big studio. Jean-Claude Carriére once wrote about the prospect of computers making films one day, his rhetorical speaker saying they most certainly would, "[and] other computers will go to see them."[2] We're subjected to—and augmented by—the "HAL Gaze." Like Douglas Adams' philosophers-on-strike in *The Hitchhiker's*

2. Carriére, *Secret Language of Film*, 211.

Guide to the Galaxy, there's the demand for demarcation when the supercomputer, Deep Thought, is programmed to do their job of the "eternal verities," answering the philosophical question of life, the universe, and everything instead of just calculating numbers. Yet Deep Thought has wrought its own supercomputer—the Earth. The orga/mecha binary grows curioser and curioser. The Earth as paradoxical computer program and solid terrestrial firmament is where Nicholas Hathaway glides, reads, authors, shoots, breaks arms, and makes love. The man is here, yes, but the machine is everything, everywhere.

Blackhat opens on a planet looking like a spider's glowing neon egg-sack. As Hoover's virtual blueprint now stretches across the entire globe, the film's opening—lap dissolves moving closer to the planet before settling on a nuclear power plant in China—is a nod to Mann's fellow Chicagoan Philip Kaufman's classic 1978 remake *Invasion of the Body Snatchers* (an important predecessor to *They Live* as well). In that case the camera doubled for descending extraterrestrial bacteria colonizing bodies and changing the species, but in *Blackhat* it's the phenomenon of the camera itself, capturing and storing and compartmentalizing, geography rewritten as binary code and absorbed into a virtual panopticon, a new kind of bodily invasion that modifies—if not fully alters—the human.[3]

3. The following analysis of *Blackhat* is based on the theatrical cut released in January 2015. On February 11, 2016, Mann screened a *Blackhat* "revision" at the Brooklyn Academy of Music. This version reverted back to Morgan Davis Foehl's original screenplay structure, placing the nuclear reactor attack toward the middle of the film, and focusing on the Chicago Stock Exchange attack at the beginning. This original structure makes a lot more sense, and one wonders if Mann's motives for changing it had less to do with "upping the stakes" at the beginning than with trying to promote a thriller having to do with soy futures. The one-and-only revision screening garnered a positive reaction from the attending audience, and in 2017 it aired on the FX

In a sense we see a world of which Dziga Vertov dreamed, the idea being that one of the few ways to truly capture "life unawares" in a movie was for people to be so accustomed to the presence of cameras on every street corner that they would eventually act naturally. But instead of utopian accomplishment, the theater of the mind is replaced by the invasive cataloging of images, spaces, and people. In Vertov's *Man with a Movie Camera* (1929), the camera was unimpeded, photographing trains from below, waking up and getting dressed with people, following them into cavernous mines, witnessing their marriages, divorces, and even their children being born, increased frame rates savoring bodies in motion, ingenious editing compressing different cities into one progressive city of the future, the microcosm inseparable from the macrocosm, opening human eyes cross-cutting with window shades and so exemplifying Vertov's idea of the "Kinok," a Russian word compounded of other words for "cinema," "eye," and "window," the conjoining of human optics and machinery resulting in a "new man" and a new way of looking, a cosmically enthusiastic transparent camera-eye cataloging cities and the "body electric" as Vertov read in one of his heroes, Walt Whitman, whose *Leaves of Grass* he carried with him at all times. A horizon opens beyond human limitations and the cinema keeps on opening, the camera eventually walking on its own and taking a bow for the audience. We can see ourselves, plainly, "unawares" as Vertov says, and are unlocked and enlightened to the cause of revolution and the new world.

The camera in *Public Enemies* is of paramount significance, used by journalists covering Dillinger's custody, relaying international information in newsreels, and being

network as the film's television premiere. However, there are as of yet no plans for releasing the film on disc or streaming service.

a handy propaganda tool for Hoover. In *Blackhat*, the cameras are now everywhere with even greater elasticity—but where is the eponymous "man" from Vertov's classic film? The image frames entire planets and then undergoes fission toward infinitesimal smallness, the physical lens vestigial as 3-D graphic design traverses from the planetary God's-Eye-View to the components of microprocessors, deeper and deeper through its inscrutable automation. The world is compressed within cyberspace, the miniscule currents having huge ramifications on the vestigial physical geography and its bodies. The film's prologue seems mutually influenced by the Burpleson Air Force Base opening of Kubrick's *Dr. Strangelove* and *2001*'s Star Gate sequence. It centers on this nuclear facility's corrupted operational systems, leading to a catastrophic meltdown. Like *Dr. Strangelove* and *2001*, human intelligence feels insignificant in command centers of automation. The drama and dialogue is in the machines (through drone sound effects that seem to be "talking"), continuing into the next hack on the other side of the globe, the camera panning over an empty trade floor in Chicago. On screens, we see that soy futures have absurdly risen. Again, human beings are disposable, their frantic bidding on trading floors driven by corrupted information in the machinery, some livestock on a television having more precedence than they do. The tone of this opening section—and much of the film—recalls a line between *Miami Vice*'s leads as they tread through a barren urban district, "Where'd all the people go?"

People are part of the "writing," and in turn the world people see is impressed with reverberations of their technological conditioning. *Blackhat* frustrates with its stubborn refusal to develop characters and spaces according to the established rules of motivation and action. The postmodernism condition killed the "author" as we knew him, and this is a new writer. While Mann gives *Blackhat*'s characters a "history," their backgrounds are repeatedly voiced through the prism of official documentation and restricted to institutional affiliations, similar to how Dillinger sees his late colleagues posted up on the Chicago Police Department's walls, more as processed numbers than human beings with family, friends, and memories.

After the cyber attacks, the Department of Justice tepidly agrees to work with the Chinese government and their cybercrime specialist, Captain Chen Dawai (Leehom Wang). DOJ supervisor Henry Pollack (John Ortiz) and FBI Agent Carol Barrett (Viola Davis) do their homework on him: Dawai's grandfather was a Shanghai military commander in the 1920s and '30s, fighting against the Japanese through the Civil War, and his father was China's Undersecretary for Trade to the UN. Dawai went to high school in New York and then college at MIT, and is now "a rising star" in the People Liberation's Army cyber defense section. Dawai insists they recruit Nicholas Hathaway (Chris Hemsworth), currently in a Pennsylvania prison for hacking into several banks and racking up $46 million. Assembled, the team's first leads in the Chicago Board of Trade firewall center have them focus on a former employee who manually plugged in the viral code, Alonso Reyes (Manny Montana). We're told that Reyes, whose identity is discerned by Barrett's recognition of his gang tattoos, did two years in prison for carding and, after getting paroled, moved to Los Angeles. Later in the story, the DOJ team runs a surveillance on the blackhat's suspected liaise, Elias Kassar (Richie Koster), who we're told fought with Christian Phalangists in the Lebanese Civil War, and then "popped up in the '90s with the paramilitaries in Columbia."

All of these details denote nothing of inner lives, and historically negate how "fraught with background," to use

Erich Auerbach's phrase, is the reference to religious and political variables. "Official" records are read off with mug shots and documented fingerprints on a screen, but the question is whether the camera, and audience, can place the fractals together and construct someone who is more than "data." We're stuck on the "writing" in the documents or read on a screen (or on their bodies), reinforced when Barrett threatens trade executive Gary Baker (Spencer Garrett), who questions the ethics of turning over trader records to the FBI and China without probable cause, with headlines on CNN that will say he's being investigated for fraud. The abstract headline, "M-Tech Official Investigated for Aiding and Abetting Cyber Criminals," hurled into an informational echo chamber with Gary Baker's photograph on the nightly news, ensures real world consequences for him. Barrett asks if she's being "tangible enough," and in this paradigm (set in place in Barrett's world by the suspender of habeas corpus, J. Edgar Hoover), she is. The world is pattern recognition and automatic information processing, the stuff of advertising.

The private histories of these characters, however, are resistant to the draconian digital cataloging the camera records, *Blackhat* inheriting the wistful intimacy of *Public Enemies*' closing message of "bye, bye blackbird." The fractals Mann gives us, if we pay attention, communicate how "fraught with background" Hathaway is, and how sacrosanct is his relationship to that history, his withholding of it a form of resistance to the discipline-and-punish panopticon surrounding him in prison, which he understands follows him outside on his furlough (notice his anger on realizing he and Dawai's sister Chen Lien [Tang Wei], brought on as a network engineer, are being observed by a security camera, remotely controlled thousands of miles away, in a Korean restaurant; Kassar has a similarly terse rage bubbling upon understanding the Chinese authorities' surveillance on him). When his cell is subjected to search, Hathaway protests on seeing his books and personal photographs callously tossed and trampled by militaristic boots. Later, in post-coital intimacy with Lien (the rhythm of which is very much like the first love scene between Dillinger and Frechette in *Public Enemies*), the director—occupier of the most voyeuristic of professions—seems to respect his character's privacy. The sound fades in and out as Hathaway lays out his youth, telling her that he was raised by a single father, a steel-worker who got sick soon after Hathaway began his prison sentence. We hear Hathaway say that in prison he would replay memories so that he could orient himself whenever he got out. Mann doesn't flashback to images of Hathaway as a young man, or even to the photographs we saw in his cell, but rather on Hathaway in prison solitary (the place where the system struggles to rewrite *you*). Elsewhere, Dawai asks Lien to be his network engineer because a blood relative is the only person he could trust during his DOJ liaison, and most dramatically, Barrett's professional breach to help Hathaway hack the NSA and illegally download the super-software, "Black Widow," has to do with what she's *seen*—the devastation of a nuclear meltdown—leaping over the isolated vacuum and evoking the day she lost her husband: September 11, 2001.

Its hero scooped out of monochrome prison and thrown into a mysterious world of rapid decision making, *Blackhat* is the cinema of the gamer, not differentiating dimensions of cyber and meat-space, the hero Hathaway being himself a video game "avatar"—Marvel's muscly Thor, Chris Hemsworth—who's a master of cyber language and yet conspicuously "meat" with a superior physique. He exercises his mind through reading (his bookshelf holds a kind of ideological gate key to the film, with Foucault's

Discipline and Punish, Lyotard's *The Postmodern Condition*, Derrida's *The Animal That Therefore I Am*, Baudrillard's *America*, Nual Phar Davis' dual biography of Oppenheimer and Lawrence, and Brian Greene's string-theory book, *The Elegant Universe*). Mann is playing with fantasies of the gamer's self-invention, and perhaps nodding to Cameron's *Avatar*, where the paraplegic gets his legs, finds love, soars through clouds, and saves the world. *Blackhat*'s cyber world is a game of illusion referenced by a climactic Balinese Hindu parade at the conclusion, an invocation of how the material world is the countenance for the unseen real world of gods and demons. At the same time, Mann's focus on environment and tangible detail is impeccable, the humidity of his locales seeping through the screen.

Hathaway is not the geeky emaciated hacker with whom we're familiar. David Fincher's cybernetic geniuses Mark Zuckerberg (Jesse Eisenberg) in *The Social Network* and Lisbeth Salander (Rooney Mara) in *The Girl With the Dragon Tattoo* were similarly fraught with history (Salander's "Fuck You You Fucking Fuck" t-shirt is the character's curt response to being "read" and textualized in a patriarchal society). History, for them, are vestigial impressions (impressed cruelty, in the case of Salander, the victim of abuse), almost similar to the "memories" Sean Young's replicant recalls in Ridley Scott's *Blade Runner*, one of Fincher's important influences, evoked in Trent Reznor and Atticus Ross's scores, and Salander's eye-makeup in one scene meant to recall Darryl Hannah's insurgent replicant. From one angle, in part influenced by Donna Harraway's feminist "Cyborg Manifesto," the way of the cyborg is a transformative path subverting the status quo's hidebound definitions of identity—and accordingly Fincher's digitalism supplants the beclouded historical determinism of analog thinking, the strictures of the body; *The Social Network* expresses this change with its humorous Grieg-synth portrayal of the fleshy Winklevoss twins (Armie Hammer, duplicated by digital ingenuity) lose their rowing competition as Zuckerberg's social media network becomes a reality—the celebrated masculine body losing its hierarchical dominance.

Conversely, Mann's embrace of the digital is a paradoxical realization of tactile historical and spatial phenomenology, lucidly picturing an end of identity while leaping, as through faith, toward the possibility of individuation in nature, free from institutional conscriptions and the negative assignations of cybernetics. While we're invited to follow Zuckerberg and Salander into the future, the dissonances of *Blackhat* and its historical burdens demands *we* read and write, digging through the binary code and imagining an MIT cyber genius "who traded in academia for gladiator academy," and like so many other Michael Mann characters found himself surrounded by new teachers and comrades, honing skills with weaponry like Frank in *Thief*, Neil and his gang in *Heat*, and of course John Dillinger, whose character is a similar hybrid of penology and media. During his brutal arraignment, a tattooed prisoner refers to Hathaway as a "carnal," a nickname of camaraderie in Hispanic prison gangs, later used by Hathaway himself over Alonso Reyes' corpse, suggesting an unlikely kinship between two inmates of different ethnicities and backgrounds nevertheless processed as equals within a penological meat-grinder.

As with the question of identity, the film prompts us to ask where nature ends and the virtual begins. *Blackhat's* myriad computer monitors of green and black smear into its physical spaces, screen-glares following the action into the real, in addition to surreal, unsettling "flaws" in the sound and image, smoothness tripping up as if to reboot and buffer. The prop of Green's *Elegant Universe*, the evocation of the unifying string theory of everything, is not arbitrary.

Dimensions co-exist here, the fusion of the virtual and tactile along with the tension between absolute control and aberrant contingency, the benevolent universe of Einstein reaching out for its reconciliation with the unpredictability of Niels Bohr's quantum mechanics (which emerged with 1920s modernity). Bodies are adoringly celebrated by Mann's camera, the movement of which evokes an idea of an intelligence and human *presence*, while disembodied surveillance cameras diminish them. Mediation is within the medium itself, Mann's technique—brilliantly analyzed by critic Ignatiy Vishnevetsky—drawing in the camera as a participant with the performers. As Vishnevetsky notes of Mann's digital period, "No one else has shots so *actorly*, expressing in grand gestures but all small nuances,"[4] something that corresponds to Vertov's use of the cameraman as an actor in *Man with a Movie Camera*. Even in the film's 3-D CGI opening, the aspiration of the virtual image is to stress the world's subatomic particle foundation, the rapid whooshing of the image not influenced by other trendy cyber movies but a blatant intertextual allusion to the opening of Krzysztof Kieslowski's classic of interconnectivity and voyeurism, *Red* (1994), a profile close-up of Hathaway in the Koreatown restaurant being an evocation of Iréne Jacob in *Red*'s poster image, a fashion advertisement that prompts us to consider the camera-eye and its subject, and the separation of the public and the private.

 Blackhat is bodies and disembodiment, corporeal truth and advertising peeking in, like we see through the DOJ team's windows in Hong Kong. *Blackhat*'s emphasis on the camera and its subsumed bodies leads back to Vertov's questions of cinema: Are we seeing real reality? Projected reality? Recorded reality? As with Mann exploding the period countenance of *Public Enemies*, Mann's choice of

4. Vishnevetsky, "Dispatches from *Public Enemies*, Part 1."

optics can vacillate from the urgency of time—as during Hathaway's sharp-edged brawl with ambushing Koreatown thugs in the restaurant—and its relativity—as during a car explosion shot at 110 frames-per-second. It's a film that in its fractious obtuseness and withholding of information contains the precariousness of space and physics, its characters traversing the globe in compressed time, the fission of the microprocessor sequences oddly doubled by lateral scans of enormous skyscrapers and the death of a marshal (Holt Mc-Callany) by gunfire, the most peculiar, and ruthless, filmic representation of a body helplessly moving through space. In Mann's hands, the cyber thriller genre becomes one of the most emphatic depictions of bodies affected in time by smaller physical particles. *Blackhat* optically savors fingers typing and code running across monitors, a striking angle underneath a keyboard perhaps nodding to a similar shot of a typewriter in Pedro Almodòvar's homoerotic thriller (similarly featuring "writing" affecting "reality") *Law of Desire* (1987). A key to decrypt the malicious hacker's data is physically possessing a corrupted hard-drive, which means Hathaway's team must go inside the dangerously radiological nuclear facility to recover it. Every second and every movement is detrimental (the body can sustain the extreme heat for only so long). The camera and montage elevate movement, such as Hathaway swinging a fire axe to open a compartment holding the drives (like Eisenstein's seminal plate smash in *Battleship Potemkin*), his thickly gloved hand plucking out the hard drive captured with hurried fixation. The scene is reminiscent of *2001*'s Bowman shutting down HAL but the machine, like radiation at the reactor site, is porous with people.

The villain of the film, "sdksdk" or "Sadek" (Yorick van Wageningen), is a self-described "gamer" with no regard or respect for the material world. His philosophy equals his mode as a character, which is peculiar for Mann, whose antagonists are incredibly formidable. Sadek can scoop up $74 million through one hack, meltdown a nuclear power plant in another, his grand scheme to flood a Malaysian riverbed so he can profit off tin shares—and so, as Hathaway notes to Lien as the camera stresses the *presence* of geography, destroying villages, village people, and village dogs. Sadek is the mischievous boil emerging from corporate capitalism's chrome-minded body, where human beings are statistics and, as stressed through *Blackhat*'s imagery at several points (particularly during the tremendous mid-film shootout between the teams of Hathaway and Kassar), part of the cargo and freight surrounding them. "Sometimes I wake up and I don't know who I am, where I am, in what country," Sadek says. "If I stop thinking about anything, it disappears. It vanishes. It ceases to exist." His zero sum methodology, thriving in the virtual world, is without conscience, keeping the real world in zeroes and ones as he refers to murder as "sub-symbolic stuff" that he delegates to his mercenary employees. It's reflected in the DOJ and Chinese government reneging their contract with Hathaway, disregarding his real-world accomplishment in locating the hacker because of his break with protocol, and because trade relations are more important than lives or dialogical contracts. However, real-world Sadek, estranged from his cyber game, is humorously feeble. His antecedents in Mann are Leo in *Thief* and Van Zandt in *Heat*, dangerous corporate criminals who are helpless outside of corporate parameters. The film's true master "antagonist" is not human at all, but the encapsulating virtual panopticon itself, humming and immense and nameless, setting a condition that disallows any time for human grief. It alerts us to its presence in the cold arena of corrupted machinery and in the callousness of Sadek, creeping into the grid of the film and how it surrounds its characters in its "erratic" writing of image and sound, interrupting from time to time, such as when Pollock resists empathy with Barrett's arguments to protect Hathaway, his institutional orders doubled by the scope of the image's virtual panoptical boundaries, as we see a peculiar cut from one angle of him saying, "Bring [Hathaway] in!" to a repetition of the same line from an angle with the camera looking at him from a slightly adjacent perspective, a jarring break in film grammar showing how infinitesimal the web of control is around characters. Though Hathaway and Lien escape "off the map" by the end of the picture, there's an uneasy sense of capture, the cinematic third-person perspective becoming a black and white security image in the chrome Argos of globaltarianistic surveillance.

Mann's cinema celebrates the materiality of existence, readjusting human nature not to given information, but what's seen and felt, the rapture of sensation, reading life as an *immersion* in it. *Blackhat* offers this when Hathaway leaves prison and luxuriates in the open space, the camera in tandem with him as it focuses on Lien's hands on his arm, and then later in a car, Hathaway's eyes silently exploring her body with nourishing fascination.[5] Their sex scene ostensibly comes out of nowhere, but it's grounded on this fresh perspective with which audiences are unaccustomed in the linearity they're usually offered romance. Like Dillinger and Frechette in *Public Enemies*, it's a transcendental

5. Between *Public Enemies* and *Blackhat*, Mann directed the pilot for David Milch's HBO racetrack series *Luck* (2012), the central character being gangster "Ace" Bernstein (Dustin Hoffman), fresh out of prison, looking to get back in the game. Bernstein's opening scene is vintage Mann, as he is being processed within the confines of prison, his eyes looking at the open light that waits for him, a blinding white that he stares at with paralyzed anticipation.

form of lovemaking tied more to the eyes than sex organs, simultaneously ridiculous and natural.

In *Blackhat*'s virtual suffocation, bodies are hungry for each other, but this intimacy carries itself into the film's depictions of violence. In a textual world run on automation, Hathaway stages a kind of primitive insurgency against Sadek's ideology, wrapping himself in text (using magazines as a kind of body-armor, a prison combat technique) and arming himself with basic tools: screwdrivers. He finds Sadek in Jakarta's Papua Square and stalks him underneath a statue celebrating Indonesia throwing off western colonialism's shackles (suggesting Hathaway's revolt against this zero-sum cyber panopticon worldview), during a Hindu ceremony where paraders walk with torches, a human scale restaging of the prologue's microprocessor sequence. Hathaway confronts his prey and, prison-style, shanks him several times through the chest—death by human touch— the hero mastering real space and time to get close enough, fast enough. Hathaway is an ideal fusion for Mann, a master of tools primitive and cybernetic.

The virtual demon materializes as a blood sacrifice, the body-to-body energy a spectacular display of the human form converging with the image, overshadowed by ageless gods in a ritual parade, living, bleeding, breathing, and dying.[6] In *Blackhat*, the camera marvels like a newborn

6. A Mann film to which *Blackhat* may have the deepest relation is arguably *The Keep* (1983), a gothic fairy tale about Nazis encountering an ancient golem-like monster in a Romanian pass. There are frequent juxtapositions between the Nazis' machinery and the surrounding countryside, and the ideological, geopolitical evil set wild with genocide in World War II is encountering its supernatural double. As with *Blackhat*, the Nazis, terrorized by the monster, bring a concentration camp prisoner, Dr. Kuza, (Ian McKellan) to help them understand what they're dealing with. The infirm, wheelchair-bound Kuza forms a Faustian pact with the golem, the master materialist given strength and revitalized by a creature of an inverse non-space.

eye at tangible surfaces and how each image—like the objects within them, such as the impact of a truck falling several dozen feet onto a building below—contains multitudes. Consider the relationship between Barrett's eyes catching sight of a looming tower above: she's just been shot squarely in the chest, life quickly draining from her as she's paralyzed to protest. The spatial distance between subject and object carries a staggering, however muted, impact on the viewer, a cargo of reference to Barrett's private grief and the more cosmological, indecipherable nature of phenomenology. This brief moment in time, like Dillinger in the Biograph, works multilaterally in how we encounter and cognitively have dialogue with the image, celebrating the audience's optical deductive tools. *Blackhat*'s gamer structure and form may rank amongst the most unique released widely in American multiplexes in recent memory—for which it wasn't rewarded, as a box office bomb and critical punching bag—and there's method to Mann's technique. He reaches for the new while stalwartly planted on the solid earth, his vision focused inward and outward, trying to reconcile the paradox and find a new way of *seeing*.

Meanwhile, the mysterious Glaeken (Scott Glenn), with inexplicable ties to the golem, arrives to stop the creature from escaping. Glaeken has sex with Kuza's daughter (Alberta Watson) that is incredibly similar in structural design to Hathaway and Lien in *Blackhat*, founded on Glaeken's similar need, as a supernatural being, to have human sensation and connection. Mann's ambitions for *The Keep* to be a dreamlike fairy tale meant resisting explaining the origins and ends of the many plot points, the film's affect being primarily visceral; also like *Blackhat*, when characters move exposition ahead through dialogue scenes, there's an errant hiccup of awkwardness. While *The Keep* is arguably unfinished (unlike his other films, Mann has no intention of revising it), its lapses into pure cinema abstraction in conjunction with its dreamlike content anticipate the formal terrain Mann would cover in his digital period.

*

Public Enemies' two movie theater scenes alluded to the importance of active dialogue with images. In *Blackhat* the seeping images drown viewers in surveillance, flowing forth while unseen, like racetrack footage on a background television strangely in focus as Hathaway's group speaks in the foreground. The world is image, virtual game, and illusion, and the question is where reciprocal dialogue can be found. Like the NSA's Black Widow software that reconstructs deleted data, the audience has to do its own supercomputing in reading the "writing on the wall," so to speak. And as code, everything in the film is "writing." The RAT (Remote Access Tool) that infiltrates cyber systems is "writing" stolen by the malicious hacker, originally written by Hathaway and Dawai at MIT, and described as "lean and graceful," its appropriator changing it to something "erratic" to achieve his ends. Hathaway and his hacker nemesis are authors of events, gods remaking the world (and so fitting that Mann should include an anachronistic religious chant on the soundtrack). Characters are themselves "writing," speaking as characters in a game, relying on idioms and verbal posturing ("What ideas are you bringing to the dance?" "When did we decide to switch goal posts?" "Our boy will bring down the big hammer." "You're dead meat." "Keys to the kingdom." "Piss off and die, ghostman," etc.). They have to be "read," and Hathaway is a master reader (he's introduced to the camera reading a book), playing word games with a sneering Department of Justice official offering a furlough contract ("Why don't you stick that contract up your ass?" "I'm sorry?" "Why are you sorry? I insulted you, I'm not sorry.") and brilliantly "reading" a Malaysian riverbed so he can deduce the hacker's next big hit, punctuated with one of civilization's most wonderful idioms, "you son of a bitch."

In this jungle of words is there any reciprocal dialogue? "There is no discussion," Dawai's PLA bosses tell him, when they demand he hand Hathaway over to the United States— a Mannian line first heard by Leo in *Thief* and suggested by Purvis's mouth behind prison bars in *Public Enemies*. *Blackhat*'s 3-D microscopic opening reveals the incredible possibilities of the digital fabric and its elegant universe, where everything is vulnerable to the eye. But the sterile institutional confines, derivative of Hoover's cyber fascist infrastructure, demonstrate the indifferent part of invention that discounts reciprocity and human value, reducing bodies to Strangelovian "human megadeaths." The digital horizon is somewhat syncretic with the atomic age, our technology reaching a new apex that, however ingenious, represents a Pandora's box with which we can't keep up and renders the world of evolved human relations incomprehensible. The form and peculiar flow of *Blackhat* manifests a rejection of the totality of globaltarian accomplishment, which I believe is one of the reasons many audiences found it abrasively inaccessible. Just as *Public Enemies* refused to present an elegant past with which we were comfortable, subverting the conventions of period costume drama, *Blackhat*'s scenic aerials are juxtaposed by its incisive, independent, fractured images and characters, not only refusing to adapt the Google-Earth clean survey of space, but the Hollywood star vehicle, with which an audience quickly orients in a fiction, guided by iconic familiarity. Hemsworth is an avatar of gifted poise and physical presence, but leagues removed from Mann's previous starring collaborators: Depp, Bale, Foxx, Farrell, Smith, Crowe, Pacino, De Niro, Day-Lewis, Caan. The plentiful supporting players fulfill their duties but are fragmented portraits: our first human point of view is Dawai, tragically killed in a car explosion before the film's fourth act; the villain Sadek is a meager Oz, a somewhat pathetic man behind his virtual curtain; and of course Barrett, played by the fantastic Viola Davis, whose death scene and final point-of-view may be the most sublime series of shots in the picture. The audience, typically coddled by images, is like fish-out-of-water Hathaway, hanging on by his fingernails in a constantly alternating environment, the locales quickly shifting from China to Chicago to Los Angeles to Hong Kong to Malaysia to Jakarta. Like Hoover's cyber command in *Public Enemies* and the global cartels in *Miami Vice*, "it's too goddamn fast," quoting the latter film. As *Blackhat* ends with its hiccupping black-and-white surveillance image of Hathaway and Lien, a question lingers of how we'll keep up with this "kamera" prison. There is no time to grieve.

Like *Public Enemies*, *Blackhat* feels like an outlier and antithetical gesture to popular currents of digital moviemaking. Of course, the six years between Mann's films were in part molded by James Cameron's *Avatar*, a manifesto displaying the limitations of the human body and meatspace, functioning as a meta-experience for its audience in a gamer's arena. Human flesh merges with technology in a singularity satisfying our deepest aspirations. Inverse to Mann's tactile sensibility, *Avatar* is also a new way of seeing, where the rubbery CGI gloss engages our eyes in an unfamiliar and palpable way: the illusion of metaphysics becomes physics, and so a miracle when the paraplegic hero finds his legs in a virtual character, Cameron's fantasy subverting the *Oz* scenario by refusing to go back to earth, the futurist philosopher understanding that we *cannot*. Jean-Baptiste Thoret writes of the film's ethos mirroring our own, "[It] is only through illusion that we can live: only the artificial is true and desirable. Who cares if humanity has to be eliminated? And what are we anyhow, if not cripples of the real—incapable of living outside those imaginary worlds called Facebook, Second Life, MSN, Match.com, Twitter, and Pandora?"[7] While several filmmakers cling to celluloid, Cameron celebrates the changing medium, his Pandora extraterrestrials literally "wired into" their cosmos, interconnected with each other in a natural (though explicitly computer-created) backdrop of primitive ritual, the director's transhumanism anticipating a grand narrative elevating a "new" human being as spiritus into the air, while the rapacious vestiges of the species are ushered back down to a dying planet.

7. Thoret, *Talk About Cinema*, 141.

CONCLUSION: A GOD'S EYE VIEW

While for many viewers *Public Enemies* evaporated as a digital misstep, *Avatar* signaled a paradigm shift, prompting theaters to completely abandon 35mm projection and be 3-D capable. Other directors followed suit: Martin Scorsese (*Hugo*), Steven Spielberg (*The Adventures of Tin Tin*), Ridley Scott (*Prometheus*), and Ang Lee (*Life of Pi*) all making bold contributions. And yet years after *Avatar*'s release, Cameron's triumph has become somewhat ambivalent, the film itself, while an enormous box office success, somewhat forgotten, the director's planned sequels in production but not with ardorous anticipation on the part of the popular audience. While the virtual 3-D dream was aggrandized in 2010, the mandate for its implementation has been limp; viewers binge on streaming television shows rather than face multiplex clamor. While 3-D immerses, there yet may be a greater impact from some independence from the image, the true dialogue and *mysterium coniunctionis* of movie alchemy occurring through open spaces separating optics from the illusion. Compare *Avatar*'s fantasy realm to Wes Anderson's *Moonrise Kingdom* (2012), where the precocious teenager Suzy (Kara Hayward) is a voracious reader of fantasy novels, upon which she builds her own inward "secret universe." She alerts us with her eyes, her glare keeping us at a distance and protecting the intimacy of that hidden world. Consequently her love story with khaki scout Sam (Jared Gilman) affects the viewer upon reflection of what they see and keep hidden, what they understand privately within public axioms, subverting "Social Services." It's a 3-D fantasy and new world myth (replete with allusions to Genesis and Noah's Ark), but the third dimension for us is in memory, like with Dillinger seeing Billie in Myrna Loy, the mystery of what the filmmaker doesn't show but what *we* nevertheless see.

*

The unsettling abrasion between the endless possibilities of digital creation and our memories is integral to the audience's collective discontentment with George Lucas and Steven Spielberg revisiting their seminal blockbusters, the *Star Wars* prequels (1999, 2002, 2005) and *Indiana Jones and the Kingdom of the Crystal Skull* (2008). The eye could not reconcile what had happened to the image in the gap of twenty-five years, as practical material effects from the 1970s and 1980s became weightless animation—a burden that *Avatar*, which is pure futurism, did not have.

There's an interpretive argument that Spielberg, who shot *Crystal Skull* on 35 mm (and continues to use film), acknowledges this, as Indiana Jones is like a Rip Van Winkle waking up in a post-atomic world, parallel to an analog franchise hero played by Harrison Ford warping from 1989 to post-digital moviedom, when filmmakers' creation box has become godlike; accordingly, the supernatural gods of the first three films are displaced by humans assuming godlike powers and control (Oppenheimer's "I Am Become Death, Destroyer of Worlds" is quoted), and yet the desire to see everything ("the space between spaces"), as rendered possible by the technology, leads to evaporating into undifferentiated dust, as Cate Blanchett's KGB Agent Spalko does (her wish to the interdimensional creatures before death being, "I want to see everything!").[1]

Lucas's *Star Wars* prequels, molded on the fresh digital palette, are even more interesting as a self-reflexive gesture of medium-as-message, almost perversely so by its third chapter, *Revenge of the Sith*. These divisive films embody the cinema of the cyborg in conjunction with its Jedi hero Anakin Skywalker's entropy, his preceding Sith Lords precipitating his trajectory as they move from real-time martial artist (Ray Park's Darth Maul) to computer augmented octogenarian (Christopher Lee's Count Dooku) to fully realized digital being (General Grievous), before ending with Anakin's metamorphosis into the machine man Darth Vader. The beautiful Renaissance boy (Hayden Christensen's appearance strikingly resembles the beautiful youth Tadzio, played by Björn Andrésen, in Luchino Visconti's *Death in Venice*) is corporeally destroyed and resurrected as a glistening masterpiece of industrial design, his vision permanently mediated by robotic viewfinders: twisted, evil, imprisoning, sterile, spiritually dead, beautiful—a new way of seeing, pinpointed much more incisively than the films' disgruntled audiences hung up on memories and countenances, oblivious to how the technology, independent of Lucas, wraps around and penetrates them, their iPhones and other gadgets also, like Darth Vader, aesthetic achievements.[2] *Blackhat* emphasizes the marvel of indus-

1. See Schwartz, "Rip Van Indy."

2. This idea, as applied to the retroactive nostalgia of Disney's current *Star Wars* sequels in relation to George Lucas's approach, is explored in my review of Rian Johnson's *The Last Jedi* (Schwartz, "Luke Warm."). Products of Disney's monoculture, it may be argued that the sequels' various directors (2015's *The Force Awakens*, 2016's *Rogue One*, 2017's *The Last Jedi*, 2018's *Solo*), working in the new corporate "Empire," are at least smuggling in a reflexivity analogous

trial design when scanning over cities, coasting through symmetries of nanotechnology, and the Chicago Trade IT room with beautiful blue lines of light making it look like a snazzy dance club. But these marvels are built for machines, the aesthetics a coincidence of their utility. Can we find spirituality in them?

Averse to Spielberg and Lucas, the master iconoclast Jean-Luc Godard quotes the Monster to Victor Frankenstein in his 3-D meditation on the image, *Goodbye to Language* (2014), "You are my creator, but I am your master—obey!" Pulling together the evolution of cinema alongside developments of nanotechnology and advertising, Godard has images expressing both great depth and barriers, the idiosyncrasies of DV's textures engaging us with the medium, our creation and monstrosity (that is to say, our *demonstrator*). "What they call images are becoming murderers of the present," we hear, background televisions stealing our attention from the foreground (featuring clips of Fritz Lang's *Metropolis* and Robert Mammoullian's *Dr. Jekyll and Mr. Hyde*, other stories suggesting the problematic paradox of invention). Godard is an unlikely kin with a Hollywood filmmaker like Mann, and yet *Blackhat* and *Goodbye to Language* are pictures struggling to hold onto a "here and now" as we notice directorial hands fidgeting with the sound and image, stridently breaking the cosmic flow with an immediacy that breaks through the screen and affects viewers. In such dissonances, is it possible our perceptions are being exercised? The world is vividly realized

---

to the more idiosyncratic creations of Lucas. Most troubling is *Rogue One*'s decision to digitally resurrect actor Peter Cushing, who died in 1994, as a nefarious imperial commander. The uncanniness of this "cyborg actor" raises ethical questions of technology's role in filmmaking, while dramatically exuding a machine-like inflexibility and post-human sensibility in step with questions posed by a text featuring artificial intelligence.

in these films, and yet the representation of reality is itself revealed as *mediation*, perhaps so that we can become more conscientious image receptors. For Godard, we complete the picture—even optically editing one scene as a 3-D image is shot *on top of* itself, our left eye becoming camera one, our right eye playing camera two. Language is hampered, yet there is a new syntax we can adopt in this labyrinth of images to help us out of a virtual prison.[3]

Godard's film reminds us that the Russian word *kamera* not only refers to a camera, but to a prison cell, pertinent to Mann's focus on panopticism and the disparity between preserving our humanity and the usefulness of tools. It's here where I return to Vertov's *kinok* ideas and link back to the intertextual reference in *Public Enemies*, when John Dillinger's eyes fastened on the dying Walter Dietrich. Dietrich's life runs out like the end of a film reel, his grasp released and movement halting to a still, the moment scored to Hans Zimmer's music from *The Thin Red Line*, directed by Terrence Malick, whom I believe is something of a kinok sibling to Michael Mann, using alchemic cinema tools to open a window and transform our perception. Whatever their differences—particularly given that Mann remains a studio filmmaker working on schedules while Malick has the privilege of working at his leisure and sculpting films in the editing room over several years—they remarkably align in how as both men grow older (they were both born in 1943) they are increasingly radical in their formal approach to the image.

There are broad similarities. Mann and Malick are both impeccable sensualists.[4] They obsess over subjectivity,

3. See Schwartz, "Godard's 3-D Monster Movie Miracle."

4. See Seitz, "Directors of the Decade," where he puts Mann and Malick together in company with Wong Kar-Wai, David Lynch, and Hou Hsiao-Hsien.

the experience of which is where personal truth is found, as opposed to objective axioms and Hegelian history. They are mutually interested in the binaries of the mechanistic and the natural, between imprisonment (socially imposed) and freedom, the flux of work and tranquil leisurely calm. They are romantics, freedom and escape personified in a love interest. Death is always waiting, often eluded but finally accepted with bold resignation, a "calm." Sometimes in flight, characters find their escape *in* death. They conscientiously fashion their own mythology, living out their myths, sometimes gracefully (Ali, Dillinger, Witt, Pocahontas), other times stridently (Kit [Martin Sheen] in *Badlands*, Baby Face Nelson, *Heat*'s Waingro). Film is consciousness, or at least the contemporary projection of consciousness, and can be utilized as either a system of projection or a system of control; in its purest form, it may lasso the "calm" for which the individual searches while evading history's obtuse assignations and officially mediated documentation, the lie of "good soldiers" like Melvin Purvis and expressed by Sgt. Welsh (Sean Penn) in *The Thin Red Line*: "They either want you dead, or in their lie."

They both emphasize communication and the vagaries of language. So much spoken dialogue is duplicitous and capricious (and for both filmmakers, often unintelligible), and sign systems wrap vines through clarion transparency. Malick has often been parodied for his use of voice-over narration, especially in his increasingly prayerful later films. But underlying Malick's Fallen Edens is the truth of language's inadequacy in its reach for the eternal. Characters ostensibly speak to each other in their voice-overs, expressing love and asking for forgiveness, but as with a prayer, the words flying up have no certain destination save the consciousness of the speaker. In Mann, dishonesty relates to a loss of speech, from where the domestic household crumbles. Corporate bodies, meanwhile, from Imperial England to the Brown and Williamson Tobacco Company, or from the United States to the Chinese government in a global economy, silence and burden people with contracts filled with guarantees that will never be fulfilled. The most honest form of communication is between two individuals sharing the here and now, self aware and aware of each other—Frank and Jessie, Hanna and McCauley, Witt and Welsh, John Smith and Pocahontas. The sand runs out, a moment slips away, and apex memories echo a sound we seek and fail to find words to articulate.

But then there is the image. In *Man with the Movie Camera*, Vertov's technique in a stringently non-narrative feature is to have the camera *register* objects, becoming a "liberation from human immobility" as the director captures reality. "Newborn. I open my eyes," begins Malick's *To the Wonder* (2013), with the director's first use of digital video, a camera phone playfully used between lovers on a train, catching their reflections before, Vertov-like, the film cuts to Emmanuel Lubezki's 35 mm third-person image, recording the recording. The camera registering is their means of communication, often fixed on characters (played—anathema to Vertov's dogma—by some of Hollywood's biggest movie stars) doing nothing but looking and listening, gazing at their gazing, the revelation of mutual adoration strangely giving these characters a soul, faces like Will Smith, Tom Cruise, Brad Pitt, Johnny Depp, Christian Bale, Cate Blanchett, Natalie Portman, Rooney Mara, and Ben Affleck appearing more unconscious of themselves as movie stars than they ever were (while appearing remarkably self-aware as fictional movie characters). A volume of information is given by a glance or a shrug. Fractions suggest a whole.

Both filmmakers' methods of communicating have evolved with media. Again while acknowledging differences, there's a lush stillness, a substantive photochemical weight to their films leading into the twenty-first century (of which Malick only had three—*Badlands, Days of Heaven*, and *The Thin Red Line*; and Mann six (theatrical features)—*Thief, The Keep, Manhunter, The Last of the Mohicans, Heat, The Insider*). Malick and cinematographer John Toll's remote controlled Akeela crane shots from *The Thin Red Line* are demarcated from the hand-held resistance to cranes in *The New World* as *Manhunter* and *Heat*'s polished canvases are from the intensified close-ups and DV of twenty-first century Mann. Bluster and noise have increased, the world is more wrapped in plain-view surveillance images, and reactantly Mann and Malick evoke Vertov in trying to find the truth, the real "God's Eye."

In *The Tree of Life* (2011), Malick's child alter ego prays as such a view overlooks a public park filled with children, "Are You watching me? I want to know what You are. I want to see what You see." Vertov's machine eye manifesto stated, "I am in perpetual motion. I approach and move away from objects—I crawl beneath them—I climb on top of them—I am even with the head of the galloping horse—I burst at top speeds into crowds—I run ahead of running soldiers—I throw myself on my back—I rise together with airplanes—I fall and fly in unison with falling and ascending bodies." Malick's opus similarly refuses to be circumscribed, as its title suggests going back to the pearl of Eden—and before that: galaxies born, planets sculpted by lava and ice, extinct creatures, not only our childhood but the uncanny sense memories of childhood dreams with marvelous specificity, and even the death of the planet and an afterlife vision.

But alongside photographed concepts is the affectation of Malick and Lubezki's impressions with wide angle lenses moving in on the subject, often to a close up, be it a face or a lamp-post. The rhapsodic dance of images, seeming to play out musically, translates through this eye and window and follows the viewer outside the theater, fast moving optics of the biological eye registering stimuli in a whole new way. *The world* is registered and contemplated by means of this canvas corresponding to the eye, "newborn," which is unimpeded, as we see it in x-rays and Skype in *To the Wonder*, and then 35 mm intermingling with GoPro footage in *Knight of Cups* (2016), *Voyage of Time* (2016), and *Song to Song* (2017), the first film including an ambient techno song by Biosphere entitled "Man with a Movie Camera," making Malick's homage and cinematic intent clearer, the roving eye moving through dead-tech modernity and advertising in search of the image Socrates speaks of in *Phaedrus*, the intimation of the eternal, the soul's wings.

The gaze is problematic (for example, the focus on bare flesh—mostly female—in *Knight of Cups* and *Song to Song* has sparked ire from certain critics). This gets back at the tension and noise between advertising, the passively consumed image, and the Platonic (and Vertovian) ideas for which Malick strives, in sync with Walt Whitman's sense of the body, which "includes and is the meaning, the main concern, and includes and is the soul . . ." *Blackhat*, with its allusion to Kieslowski's *Red* and advertising, has a similar tension, where the world can be a videoscopic dystopia of bodies processed as freight, or conversely a blessing and wonderment for the seer, the intimate alchemy of seeing liberating one from the confines of automation overload. In *Public Enemies*, a movie triggers John Dillinger's hidden muse, prompting a message from him to Billie Frechette, an exchange witnessed and carried on by *Public Enemies'* audience. It is a liminal message by means of raw materials and our gadgets, technology aspiring to the divine and struggling to affirm the significance of things we've been lucky to behold. In *To the Wonder*, a struggling priest (Javier Bardem) affirms the transcendent through the unknowable matrix of the God's Eye perspective: "Where are you leading me? Teach us where to seek you. Christ, be with me. Christ before me. Christ behind me. Christ in me. Christ beneath me. Christ above me. Christ on my right. Christ on my left. Christ in my heart." The prayer is conjoined with him seeing other people, and so clasping the camera's registry with Christ's commandment from Matt 22:39, "You *shall* love." The bodies in sight levitate as our muses, electrified and enervated, lighting up the universe.

If the image and its proliferation are, from one angle, a panopticon and prison, in their later films Michael Mann and Terrence Malick also insist on the cinema being a window, a new eye and idea, a mutual enlivener exchanged between artisan and tool prompting our senses to reach through that window, images whispering hushed but overpowering messages through the cracks of cold surveillance and disposable media, the light that spurs us on, persistently and privately, to seek lost Edens and new Jerusalems laid across inward frontiers.

BIBLIOGRAPHY

Adorno, Theodore, and Max Horkheimer. "The Culture Industry: Enlightenment as Mass Deception." From *Dialectic of Enlightenment: Cultural Memory in the Present*, 94–136. Translated by Edmund Jephcott. New York: Continuum, 1993.

Adams, Douglas. *The Hitchhiker's Guide to the Galaxy*. New York: Pocket Books, 1981.

Almodovar, Pedro, dir. *Law of Desire*. El Deseo, 1987. Film.

Anderson, Laurie, dir. *Heart of a Dog*. Canal Street Communications, 2015. Film.

Anderson, Paul Thomas, dir. *There Will Be Blood*. Paramount Vantage, 2007. Film.

Anderson, Wes, dir. *Moonrise Kingdom*. Indian Paintbrush, 2012. Film.

Aradillas, Aaron, and Matt Zoller Seitz. "Zen Pulp, Pt. 4: Do You See?: Michael Mann's Reflections, Doubles, and Doppelgangers." *Moving Image Source*. Museum of the Moving Image, July 15, 2009. http://www.movingimagesource.us/articles/zen-pulp-pt-4-20090715.

Assayas, Olivier, dir. *Clouds of Sils Maria*. IFC, 2015. Film.

Bay, Michael, dir. *Transformers*. Dreamworks, Paramount, 2007. Film.

———, dir. *Transformers: Revenge of the Fallen*. Dreamworks, Paramount, 2009. Film.

———, dir. *Transformers: Dark of the Moon*. Dreamworks, Paramount, 2011. Film.

———, dir. *Transformers: Age of Extinction*. Dreamworks, Paramount, 2014. Film.

Benjamin, Walter. *Illuminations: Essays and Reflections*. Edited by Hannah Arendt. Translated by Harry Zohn. New York: Schocken, 1968.

————. *The Work of Art in the Age of Its Technological Reproducibility and Other Writings on Media*. Edited by Michael W. Jennings, Brigid Doherty, and Thomas Y. Levin. Translated by Edmund Jephcott, Rodney Livingstone, and Howard Eiland. Cambridge: Harvard University, 2008.

Bigelow, Kathryn, dir. *Strange Days*. 20th Century Fox, 1995. Film.

————, dir. *Zero Dark Thirty*. Columbia, 2012. Film.

Burrough, Bryan. *Public Enemies: America's Greatest Crime Wave and the Birth of the F.B.I, 1933–34*. New York: Penguin, 2004.

Cameron, James, dir. *Avatar*. 20th Century Fox, 2009. Film.

Carpenter, John, dir. *They Live*. Universal, 1998. Film.

Carriére, Jean-Claude. *The Secret Language of Film*. Translated by Jeremy Leggatt. New York: Pantheon, 1994.

C. K., Louis, dir. *Horace and Pete*. Louisck.com, 2016. Television.

————, dir. *Louie*. FX, 2010–15. Television.

Cooper, Scott, dir. *Black Mass*. Warner Bros, 2015. Film.

Coppola, Francis Ford, dir. *The Conversation*. Paramount, 1974. Film.

————, dir. *The Godfather*. Paramount, 1972. Film.

————, dir. *The Godfather Part II*. Paramount, 1974. Film.

————, dir. *The Godfather Part III*. Paramount, 1990. Film.

Coppola, Sofia, dir. *The Bling Ring*. A24, 2013. Film.

————, dir. *Somewhere*. Focus, 2010. Film.

Corliss, Richard. "Kill Dill: Depp's Dillinger Disappoints." *Time Magazine*, July 6, 2009.

Costa, Pedro. *Colossal Youth*. Memento, 2006. Film.

Cronenberg, David, dir. *Cosmopolis*. eOne, 2012. Film.

Cuaron, Alfonso, dir. *Children of Men*. Universal, 2006. Film.

De Palma, Brian, dir. *The Untouchables*. Paramount, 1987. Film.

Ebiri, Bilge. "Now Is the Time to Discover Michael Mann's *Ali*." *The Village Voice*, July 14, 2016. https://www.villagevoice.com/2016/06/14/now-is-the-time-to-discover-michael-manns-ali/.

Edelman, Ezra. *O.J.: Made in America*. ESPN, 2016. Documentary.

Edwards, Gareth, dir. *Rogue One: A Star Wars Story*. Disney, 2016. Film.

Eisenstein, Sergei, dir. *Battleship Potemkin*. Goskino, Mosfilm, 1925. Film.

————. *Film Form*. Edited and translated by Jay Leyda. San Diego: Harcourt, 1979.

————. *The Film Sense*. Edited and translated by Jay Leyda. San Diego: Harcourt, 1975.

Feeney, F. X. *Michael Mann*. Edited by Paul Duncan. Los Angeles: Taschen, 2006.

Fitzgerald, F. Scott. *The Great Gatsby*. New York: Scribner, 2004.

Friedman, Roger. "*Miami Vice:* Summer's Biggest Bust?" *Fox News*, June 20, 2006. http://www.foxnews.com/story/2006/06/20/miami-vice-summer-biggest-bust.html.

———. "*Miami Vice* Theme: Axed, but Alive." *Fox News*, July 25, 2006. http://www.foxnews.com/story/2006/07/25/lsquomiami-vicersquo-theme-axed-but-alive.html.

Gibson, William. *Count Zero*. New York: Ace, 1987.

———. *Neuromancer*. New York: Ace, 1984.

———. *Spook Country*. New York: Berkeley, 2009.

———. *Zero History*. New York: Berkeley, 2011.

Gilroy, Tony, dir. *Duplicity*. Universal, 2009. Film.

———, dir. *Michael Clayton*. Warner Bros, 2007. Film.

Godard, Jean-Luc, dir. *Film Socialisme*. Wild Bunch, 2010. Film.

———, dir. *Goodbye to Language*. Wild Bunch, 2014. Film.

———, dir. *In Praise of Love*. Avventura Films, 2001. Film.

Greengrass, Paul, dir. *The Bourne Supremacy*. Universal, 2004. Film.

———, dir. *The Bourne Ultimatum*. Universal, 2007. Film.

———, dir. *United 93*. Universal, 2006. Film.

Haraway, Donna. *Simians, Cyborgs, and Women: The Reinvention of Nature*. New York: Routledge, 1990.

Jackson, Peter, dir. *The Hobbit: An Unexpected Journey*. Warner Bros, 2012. Film.

Jonze, Spike, dir. *Her*. Warner Bros, 2013. Film.

Joseph, Kahlil, and Beyonce Knowles, dirs. *Beyonce: Lemonade*. 2016. Music video.

Kelly, Richard, dir. *The Box*. Warner Bros, 2009. Film.

———, dir. *Donnie Darko*. Newmarket, 2001. Film.

———, dir. *Southland Tales*. Samuel Goldwyn, 2006. Film.

Kiarostami, Abbas, dir. *ABC Africa*. IFAD, 2001. Documentary.

———, dir. *Shirin*. Abbas Kiarostami Productions, 2008. Film.

———, dir. *Ten*. Abbas Kiarostami Productions, 2002. Film.

Kieslowski, Krzysztof, dir. *Three Colors: Red*. Miramax, 1994. Film.

Kolker, Robert. *A Cinema of Loneliness*. 3rd ed. New York: Oxford, 2000.

———. *Film, Form, and Culture*. Boston: McGraw-Hill, 1999.

Kubrick, Stanley, dir. *2001: A Space Odyssey*. MGM, 1968. Film.

———, dir. *Dr. Strangelove, or How I Learned to Stop Worrying and Love the Bomb*. Columbia, 1964. Film.

Lang, Fritz, dir. *Metropolis*. Universum Film, 1927. Film.

Lawson, Richard. "Will *Public Enemies* Be Just Another Hollow Michael Mann Movie?" *Gawker*, July 1, 2009. http://gawker.com/5305704/will-public-enemies-be-just-another-hollow-michael-mann-movie.

Lee, Ang, dir. *Life of Pi*. 20th Century Fox, 2012. Film.

Levinson, Barry, dir. *Bugsy*. TriStar, 1991. Film.

Lucas, George, dir. *Star Wars Episode III: Revenge of the Sith*. 20th Century Fox, 2005. Film.

Luzi, Evan. "Top 5 Directors Who Should've Stayed Away from Digital Filmmaking." *The Black and Blue*, March 4, 2010. http://www.theblackandblue.com/2010/03/04/top-5-directors-who-shouldve-stayed-away-from-digital-filmmaking/.

Lynch, David, dir. *INLAND EMPIRE*. Absurda, 2006. Film.

———, dir. *Mulholland Dr.* USA Films, 2001. Film.

———, dir. *Twin Peaks: The Return*. Showtime, 2017. Television.

Maccabee, Paul. *John Dillinger Slept Here: A Crooks' Tour of Crime and Corruption in St. Paul, 1920–1936*. St. Paul: Minnesota Historical Society, 1995.

Malick, Terrence, dir. *Badlands*. Warner Bros, 1973. Film.

———, dir. *Days of Heaven*. Paramount, 1978. Film.

———, dir. *Knight of Cups*. Broad Green, 2015. Film.

———, dir. *The New World*. New Line, 2005. Film.

———, dir. *Song to Song*. Broad Green, 2017. Film.

———, dir. *The Thin Red Line*. Fox 2000, 1998. Film.

———, dir. *To the Wonder*. Magnolia, 2013. Film.

———, dir. *The Tree of Life*. Fox Searchlight, 2011. Film.

———, dir. *Voyage of Time*. Broad Green, 2016. Film.

Mamoulian, Rouben, dir. *Dr. Jekyll and Mr. Hyde*. Paramount, 1931. Film.

Mann, Michael, dir. *Ali*. Columbia, 2001. Film.

———, prod. *The Aviator*. Miramax, Warner Bros, 2004. Film.

———, dir. *Blackhat*. Universal, Legendary, 2015. Film.

———, dir. *Collateral*. Dreamworks, Paramount, 2004. Film.

———, executive prod. *Crime Story*. NBC, 1986–88. Television.

———, dir. *Heat*. Warner Bros, 1995. Film.

———, dir. *The Insider*. Touchstone, 1999. Film.

———, dir. *The Keep*. Paramount, 1983. Film.

———, dir. *The Last of the Mohicans*. 20th Century Fox, 1992. Film.

———, executive prod. *Luck*. HBO, 2011. Television.

———, dir. *Manhunter*. De Laurentiis Entertainment Group, 1986. Film.

———, executive prod. *Miami Vice*. NBC, 1984–89. Television.

———, dir. *Miami Vice*. Universal, 2006. Film.

———, dir. *Public Enemies*. Universal, 2009. Film.

———, executive prod. *Robbery Homicide Division*. CBS, 2002–2003. Television.

———, dir. *Thief*. United Artists, 1981. Film.

Marcuse, Herbert. *One-Dimensional Man: Studies in the Ideology of Advanced Industrial Society*. New York: Routledge, 2002.

Masters, Kim. "Hurricane Michael." *Slate*, July 27, 2006. http://www.slate.com/articles/news_and_politics/hollywood/2006/07/hurricane_michael.html.

———. "Knives Out for Michael Mann." *The Daily Beast*, June 30, 2009. http://www.thedailybeast.com/articles/2009/06/30/public-enemies-true-crimes.html.

McLuhan, Marshall. *Understanding Media: The Extensions of Man*. Cambridge: MIT, 1994 [1964].

Mendes, Sam, dir. *Road to Perdition*. Dreamworks, 2002. Film.

Newell, Mike, dir. *Donnie Brasco*. TriStar, 1997. Film.

Olsen, Mark. "Paint It Black." *Sight and Sound* 14 (October 2006) 16. http://old.bfi.org.uk/sightandsound/feature/224.

Pabst, G. W., dir. *The Joyless Street*. Sofar-Film, 1925. Film.

Pasolini, Pier Paolo, dir. *The Gospel According to St. Matthew*. 1964. Film.

Penn, Arthur, dir. *Bonnie and Clyde*. Warner Bros, 1967. Film.

Polanski, Roman, dir. *The Ghost Writer*. Summit, 2010. Film.

Reed, Carol, dir. *Odd Man Out*. Two Cities Film, 1947. Film.

Reichardt, Kelly, dir. *Certain Women*. IFC, 2016. Film.

———, dir. *Night Moves*. Cinedigm, 2013. Film.

———, dir. *Old Joy*. Film Science, 2006. Film.

———, dir. *Wendy and Lucy*. Oscilloscope, 2008. Film.

Rybin, Steven. *The Cinema of Michael Mann*. Lanham, MD: Lexington, 2007.

Salles, Walter, dir. *The Motorcycle Diaries*. Buena Vista, 2004. Film.

Schwartz, Niles. "Body and Soul: Revisiting Michael Mann's *Ali*." *RogerEbert.com*, June 15, 2016. www.rogerebert.com/balder-and-dash/body-and-soul-revisiting-michael-manns-ali.

———. "Godard's 3-D Monster Movie Miracle: 'Goodbye to Language.'" *Minneapolis/St. Paul Cinephile Society*, March 19, 2017. https://www.mspcinephiles.org/criticism/2017/3/19/godards-3-d-monster-movie-goodbye-to-language/.

———. "Luke Warm: 'The Last Jedi.'" *Minneapolis/St. Paul Cinephile Society*, December 17, 2017. www.mspcinephiles.org/criticism/2017/12/17/luke-warm-the-last-jedi.

———. "Rip Van Indy: Reconsidering 'Crystal Skull.'" *Minneapolis/St. Paul Cinephile Society*, March 10, 2017. www.mspcinephiles.org/criticism/2017/3/18/rip-van-indy-reconsidering-crystal-skull-1.

Scorsese, Martin, dir. *The Aviator*. Miramax, Warner Bros, 2004. Film.

———, dir. *Casino*. Universal, 1995. Film.

———, dir. *The Departed*. Warner Bros, 2006. Film.

———, dir. *Goodfellas*. Warner Bros, 1990. Film.

———, dir. *Hugo*. Paramount, 2011. Film.

———, dir. *Shutter Island*. Paramount, 2010. Film.

Scott, Ridley, dir. *Blade Runner*. Warner Bros, Alan Ladd, 1982, 1992, 2007. Film.

———, dir. *Prometheus*. 20th Century Fox, 2012. Film.

Seitz, Matt Zoller. "Directors of the Decade No. 9: The Sensualists." *Salon*, December 16, 2009. http://www.salon.com/2009/12/17/sensualists_seitz/.

———. "The Unloved, Part Thirteen: *Public Enemies*." (Editor's Note). *RogerEbert.com*, January 5, 2015. http://www.rogerebert.com/mzs/the-unloved-part-thirteen-public-enemies.

———. "Zen Pulp, Pt. 3: I'm Looking at You, Miss.: The Women of Mann." *Moving Image Source*. Museum of the Moving Image, July 9, 2009. http://www.movingimagesource.us/articles/zen-pulp-pt-3-20090709.

Selznick, David O., prod. *Manhattan Melodrama*. MGM, 1934. Film.

Serra, Albert, dir. *Honor of the Knights*. 2006. Film.

Soderbergh, Steven, dir. *Behind the Candelabra*. HBO, 2013. Film.

———, dir. *Che*. IFC, 2008. Film.

———, dir. *Contagion*. Warner Bros, 2010. Film.

———, dir. *The Girlfriend Experience*. Magnolia, 2009. Film.

———, dir. *Haywire*. Relativity, 2012. Film.

———, dir. *The Informant!* Warner Bros, 2009. Film.

———, dir. *The Knick*. Cinemax, 2014-2015. Television.

———, dir. *Magic Mike*. Warner Bros, 2012. Film.

———, dir. *Mosaic*. HBO, 2018. App. Television.

———, dir. *Side Effects*. Open Road, 2013. Film.

Spielberg, Steven, dir. *The Adventures of Tintin*. Paramount, 2011. Film.

———, dir. *A.I. Artificial Intelligence*. Dreamworks, Warner Bros, 2001. Film.

———, dir. *The BFG*. Disney, 2016. Film.

———, dir. *Indiana Jones and the Kingdom of the Crystal Skull*. Paramount, 2008. Film.

———, dir. *Lincoln*. Disney, 2012. Film.

———, dir. *Minority Report*. Dreamworks, 2002. Film.

———, dir. *Munich*. Universal, 2005. Film.

———, dir. *War of the Worlds*. Paramount, 2005. Film.

Steinbeck, John. *The Grapes of Wrath*. 1939. New York: Penguin, 2002.

Stone, Oliver, dir. *Alexander*. Warner Bros, 2004, 2005, 2007, 2014. Film.

———, dir. *Snowden*. Open Road, 2016. Film.

Tafoya, Scout. "The Unloved, Part Thirteen: *Public Enemies*." *RogerEbert.com*, January 5, 2015. http://www.rogerebert.com/mzs/the-unloved-part-thirteen-public-enemies.

Thoret, Jean-Baptiste. "The Aquarium Syndrome." Translated by Anna Dzenis & Adrian Martin. *Screening the Past*, October 2013 [2000].

———. "Gravity of the Flux: Michael Mann's *Miami Vice*." Translated by Sally Shafto. *Senses of Cinema* 42 (February 2007). http://sensesofcinema.com/2007/feature-articles-/Miami-vice/.

———. *Talk About Cinema*. Translated by David Radzinowicz. Paris: Flammarion, 2012.

Vertov, Dziga. *Kino-Eye: The Writings of Dziga Vertov*. Edited by Annette Michelson. Translated by Kevin O'Brien. Berkeley: University of California, 1984.

———, dir. *The Man with a Movie Camera*. VUFKU, 1929. Film.

Villeneuve, Denis, dir. *Blade Runner: 2049*. Warner Bros, 2017. Film.

Vishnevetsky, Ignatiy. "Dispatches from *Public Enemies*, Part 1: Dillinger is Dead." *Mubi*, June 26, 2009. https://mubi.com/notebook/posts/dispatches-from-public-enemies-part-1-dillinger-is-dead.

———. "Dispatches from *Public Enemies*, Part 2: Beyond the Time Barrier." *Mubi*, June 29, 2009. https://mubi.com/notebook/posts/dispatches-from-pubic-enemies-part-2-beyond-the-time-barrier.

———. "Dispatches from *Public Enemies*, Part 3: The Mad Masters." *Mubi*, June 30, 2009. https://mubi.com/notebook/posts/dispatches-from-public-enemies-part-3-the-mad-masters.

———. "What Is the 21st Century?: Frame-Rate Follies." *Mubi*, December 14, 2012. https://mubi.com/notebook/posts/what-is-the-21st-century-frame-rate-follies.

Wachowski, Lana, and Wachowski, Lilly, dirs. *The Matrix*; Warner Bros, 1999. Film.

———, dir. *The Matrix Reloaded*; Warner Bros, 2003. Film.

———, dir. *The Matrix Revolutions*. Warner Bros, 2003. Film.

Wildermuth, Mark E. *Blood in the Moonlight: Michael Mann and Information Age Cinema*. Jefferson, MD: McFarland, 2005.